MW01088650

First edition published November 2017

Oftwominds.com

P.O. Box 4727

Berkeley, California 94704

Interior: Jill Kanter

Cover: Theresa Barzyk

Concept and all the difficult bits: Gary F. Baker

.

Money and Work Unchained

Charles Hugh Smith

Table of Contents

INTRODUCTION 1

SECTION ONE: WORK 5

I. THE COMPLEX WEALTH CREATED BY WORK 5

What is Work? 5

The Taxonomy and Ontology of Work 14

Need as a Driving Force 22

What Makes Work Fulfilling? 27

The Impact of High-Touch / Low-Touch on Work Fulfillment 29

The Impact of Cost 31

How Do We Value Work? 36

Personal vs. Public Value of Work 36

Why Is Some Work Paid and Other Work Unpaid? 39

Core Conditions for Paid vs. Unpaid Work 41

II. THE DESERTIFICATION OF LIFE: WHEN WORK DISAPPEARS 43

Our Failed Coping Mechanisms and the Denial of Loss 46

The Loss of Social Roles and Meaning 49

The Emptiness of Consumerism 52

The Loss of Local Production and Social Cohesion 54

III. THE FANTASY WORLD OF UNIVERSAL BASIC INCOME 58

The Core Tenets of Universal Basic Income 58

The Three Arguments in Favor of UBI 60

The Implicit Assumption: The Elite Class is Superior 61

What Do the Wealthy Have That the Poor Don't Have? 62

UBI's Embrace of Infinite Growth on a Finite Planet 67

UBI's Embrace of a Fraudulent Financial System 69

The Impracticalities of UBI 70

Misunderstanding the Economics of Robots 71

Robots Will Only Perform Work That Is Profitable 77

Where Will the Trillions for UBI Come From? 80

UBI's Consequences: Dependence, Social Depression, Inflation and Debt-Serfdom 85

Emotional Appeal Is Not a Substitute for Practical Policy 91

The Fantasy of Creative Self-Expression Replacing Work 92

The Democratization of Artistic Expression 94

The Fantasy of Paid Work from Creative Self-Expression 99

The Fantasy of Subsidized Entrepreneurship 101

Universal Basic Income's Dependence on Maximizing Profits 106

Meaningful Work Is Wealth; the Demand for High-Touch Work . 109

IV. THE STRUCTURAL FAILURE OF THE CURRENT MODE OF PRODUCTION 111

What's Broken? 111

What's Scarce? 113

The Current System Has No Mechanism to Differentiate Fundamentally Different Things 114

The Wrong Unit Size and the Wrong Structure 116

The Internal Logic of the Current Mode of Production 118

The False Promise of Ever-Expanding Profits via Automation 123

Limits on the State Paying for Unprofitable Work 138

A New Mode of Production 139

SECTION TWO: MONEY **141**

THE LIMITS OF OUR SOCIAL CONSTRUCT OF MONEY 141

What Is Money? 141

The Functions of Money 142

Our Money System Enforces Inequality 144

The Key Characteristics of Our Social Construct of Money 147

Why Money Loses Purchasing Power, a.k.a. Inflation 152

Our Reliance on Expanding Debt 155

The Fantasy of a Free Money Machine 157

The Intrinsic Instability of State and Private-Bank Issued Credit-Money *159*

SECTION THREE: A NEW RELATIONSHIP BETWEEN WORK AND MONEY **163**

Good Ideas Don't Require Force *165*

The Role of Cryptocurrencies in a New Mode of Production *165*

Enabling Sustainable Commerce that Fills Scarcities That Cannot Be Profitably Filled *167*

The Outline of a New Mode of Production *168*

Introduction

Do we understand work and money? Most of us would probably answer "yes."

- Work is what we do to earn money.
- Money is what we earn from work, and what we use to buy things we want or need.

But is that all work is—a way to earn money? And is that all money is, something we use to buy things?

Or do we just think we understand work and money simply because they are commonplace features of everyday life?

Work is actually much more than a way to earn money, and money is much more than a means to buy things. The two are key to understanding *wealth*, which is also much more than just *an abundance of money*.

Money and work are also key to understanding *capital*, which is more than the conventional definition of tools, commodities, stocks, bonds and real estate.

The title of this book is *Money and Work Unchained*. You may assume I mean unchaining money *from* work, but in reality, money is already disconnected from work. Consider the following: if I borrow $1 billion at 1% interest, and invest this money in a bond yielding 3% interest, I would earn $20 million annually (2% of $1 billion) just for typing a few computer keystrokes.

The privilege of borrowing a large sum of money at low interest rates earned me the money, not my labor. Clearly, money is already unchained from work.

Work is also already unchained from money, as a great deal of useful work isn't paid. Indeed, a large part of all the work performed on Earth isn't paid.

What we'll be exploring is *unchaining work from our preconceptions of work* and *unchaining money from our preconceptions of money*. By freeing work and money from the shackles of our assumptions, we're free to design a more productive, sustainable and fair society with a much broader distribution of *real wealth and capital*.

So why is it important to free money, work, wealth and capital from our current conceptual assumptions?

The world has entered an age of accelerating automation that is rapidly replacing human labor. The common assumption is that this will free humans from the burdens of work, and enable millions of people the luxuries of leisure and artistic expression. This is the dream embodied by Universal Basic Income (UBI), the increasingly popular proposal to give everyone a monthly income without any strings attached.

But where will the money come from to pay us all to no longer perform productive work?

To infer that the money will come from automation's profits or by borrowing the money from future taxpayers makes erroneous assumptions about the nature of money, profit and wealth.

The danger is that if we don't fully understand work, money, wealth and capital, we may find ourselves in a *behavioral sink* of purposeless despair with no income at all. Rather than entering a paradise of paid leisure, we might find ourselves in a nightmare of social dysfunction that extends far beyond financial destitution, deep into a toxic poverty of purpose and meaning.

This book poses a thought experiment: let's assume we don't really understand work and money, and that we'll discover their nature by asking a series of questions:

- What is work?
- What role does work play in human life?
- How is work connected to money, capital and wealth?

- Once we have a better understanding of work, where does this take us?

Then we'll ask the same questions of money:

- What is money?
- What role does money play in human life?
- How is money connected to capital, wealth and work?
- Once we have a better understanding of money, where does this take us?

We also need to investigate the connections between money, work, capital and wealth:

- What are the connections between work, money, capital and wealth?
- Once we understand the connections, where does this take us?

The process of asking these questions reveals a startling truth: we naturally assume our conceptions of work and money are like laws of Nature—that our concepts are reflections of immutable characteristics of work and money.

But the reality is that our concepts are *not* laws of Nature—they are *social constructs*. And once we reach a different understanding of work and money, we can adopt entirely different social constructs that will improve our lives and communities in a sustainable fashion.

Section One: Work

I. The Complex Wealth Created by Work

What is Work?

What is work? The commonly accepted definition is "work is what we do to earn money." But since not all work is paid—a subject we'll explore in the next section—in order to truly understand work, we have to ask: other than its connection to money, what else sets work apart from the rest of human activity?

We could start by noting the obvious: that work is different from leisure. We know watching TV isn't work, but what differentiates watching TV from work? Our first answer is: *work is what someone pays us to do.* But this isn't very helpful, as a great deal of work isn't paid. Furthermore, it's not always obvious whether an activity is leisure or work.

Very few people get paid to watch TV, and those few who are paid—TV critics, for example—aren't paid solely to watch TV; they're paid to assess the content of the TV programs and prepare their assessment for media distribution.

Since nobody pays me to do yardwork around my own house, is that a leisure activity rather than work? But if I do the exact same task for my neighbor who pays me, then does this same activity becomes work?

Take a craft hobby such as assembling a quilt or fashioning a piece of furniture. The process of making a quilt or cabinet as paid work is very similar to the hobbyists' activity. If I give the cabinet I made away, then my labor was leisure, but if I sell it, then does my labor qualifies as work?

Clearly, commercial value has a role in certain kinds of work, but it doesn't help us understand the nature of work or what sets it apart from other activities.

Work has a different structure than leisure. This may seem obvious, but what makes the same activity leisure in one setting and work in another? It's not simply a matter of getting paid.

The working TV critic may appear to be no different than the person being entertained, but the process of assessing the program, comparing it to past series and competing offerings, is quite different from being entertained.

We can start by observing that work generates an *output*: some goal is reached, and the work yields some measurable value. In other words, work is focused on *production rather than consumption*. The product may have *utility value*, i.e. it's useful, or others may value the result for other reasons.

By this definition, making a quilt or piece of furniture is clearly work, regardless of the commercial value of the finished item. Both have utility value, as the quilt keeps us warm at night and the cabinet serves to store things. If the quilt and cabinet are well-made and attractive, they may also provide an aesthetic value to those using them.

We all understand utility value and aesthetic value, but what other kinds of value are created by work?

Consider two swimmers in a pool. Both are doing the same activity, but one is swimming for enjoyment, while the other is training for a team race. The first activity is leisure, the second is something different than leisure. But is it work? The swimmer who is training isn't being paid, nor is she producing a tangible item with utility or aesthetic value. Nonetheless, her training seems more like work than leisure. This example illustrates that work has intangible, invisible qualities—in this instance, *an intent and goal that sets it apart from leisure*.

The first swimmer's intent and goal is to relax via a leisurely swim; the swim's output isn't being measured, and its value to others isn't a consideration. While others may derive some value from her choice to take a swim rather than enjoy some other form of leisure, that isn't the goal or *organizing purpose* of her swim.

The point here is the *value* of an activity may be invisible to observers: the leisurely swimmer may place a high value on the relaxation and fitness benefits of her swim. Her swim may well benefit her family members and society via its health benefits, but this is quite different from the value others place on the other swimmer's training.

The second swimmer's intent and goal is to improve her lap time and endurance to increase her chances of winning team races, and this is the *organizing purpose* of her swim. She may or may not enjoy her time in the water, but her pleasure isn't the *organizing purpose* for the activity; that is not why she is swimming, nor does it inform the *structure of her swimming*.

The first swimmer can stop whenever she chooses, or switch strokes at whim; the *organizing purpose* of her swim is personal relaxation, and that purpose defines the structure of her activity: she swims for whatever time she chooses, and stops when her mental and physical state suits her.

Her activity generates health benefits, but these don't define the structure of her leisurely swim. If improved health was the *organizing purpose*, then the structure of her swim would include metrics such as her pulse rate increasing to a desired range, and her swim would have to be of a minimal duration.

In other words, if the organizing purpose is improving health in some measurable way, this requires an *intentional, sustained effort* and *measuring the output* of her activity.

This is not to say that the value of the leisurely swimmer's activity is somehow less than the value of the competitive swimmer's workout, any more than the hobbyist's furniture is less valuable than the paid craftsperson's furniture. The point is that *work is structured differently from leisure*; it has a different *organizing purpose* that requires a much different *structure* than leisure activities.

There is another key difference between the leisurely swim and the training swim: the *social value* of each swimmers' activity.

The competitive swimmer's time in the pool is structured not just to reach benchmarks such as faster lap times. Her membership on a team means that the *organizing purpose* of her time in the pool is to help her team win competitions. *The social value of the team is the core organizing purpose* of her training. The team is not just individuals who happen to compete on the same roster. The output of each member's training has value to her teammates, her coach and the team's sponsors in ways that are different from the value that others derive from the leisurely swimmer's time in the pool.

Both swimmers generate *social value*. The leisurely swimmer's physical and mental health is improved, benefiting her family and friends, and lowering the odds of chronic lifestyle diseases that burden society with higher costs of care.

The competitive swimmer's effort has value to a range of other people and institutions. If the swimmer's training results in her winning key races, her career may advance; this is a personal gain. But her coach's career—and the monetary rewards that accrue to winning coaches—may also advance. The team accrues value from her winning races, as do institutional backers of the team (a university or corporate sponsors, for example). Each member of the team gains value from her winning races as well, as there is potential career/commercial value in belonging to a winning team.

If her wins create a financially lucrative career in swimming, that result will also enhance the finances of her family.

The point here is two-fold: many other people may obtain value from each swimmers' efforts, and the *social value* created by their activity is complex and far-reaching. Secondly, *the social value of the team effort is an integral part of the second swimmer's organizing purpose* and the structure of her time in the pool. There is no equivalent formal social value in the structure and organizing purpose of the leisurely swimmer's time in the pool.

The leisurely swimmer doesn't enter the pool thinking, I'm doing this so I'll be a better spouse, Mom and colleague as a result of being fitter and more relaxed; the *organizing purpose of her swim is private.*

The competitive swimmer enters the pool remembering her coach's advice and her role in the upcoming team competition. She may be feeling the sting of a loss resulting from her previous performance. The *organizing purpose of her swim is social, i.e. the team's collaborative efforts to win competitions.*

One way to understand the difference is: *the competitive swimmer is needed* by the team, coach and sponsors. The group needs the competitive swimmer's best efforts and most diligent training. If the competitive swimmer shortens her training or slacks off, she has let the team down.

The leisurely swimmer has no comparative social need driving her activity. She can leave the pool early, or skip a day without feeling she has let someone else down. Nobody needs her to swim her best or be diligent about in her time in the pool.

That *being needed is the source of dignity and self-worth* is poorly understood in our socio-political-economic system. Yet this dynamic is core to being human: we crave not just social connections and the affection of others, but to be *needed and valued. Contributing to a purpose greater than ourselves* in ways that are valued is the glue that binds our most meaningful social relations.

Being on the team gives the competitive swimmer a *positive social role,* a publicly recognizable identity in an organization that plays a role in the community at large. In other words, being a team member is not only an *internal state* of belonging and awareness of being needed, it is a *social state* in which others know that she is on the team and that this membership is meaningful because it entails obligations to work hard, support her teammates, follow the coach's program, and so on—in other words, *contribute to a purpose greater than herself.*

A key characteristic of positive social roles is *membership in service of a purpose greater than oneself.*

The fundamental human need for a positive social role is also poorly understood in our socio-political-economic system. The system recognizes physical and financial need, and responds to these basic needs with social welfare programs such as housing vouchers, medical care and more expansively, Universal Basic Income (UBI), a proposed solution to the automation of work that we'll analyze in a later section.

But the equally fundamental need for positive social roles that provide purpose, meaning, dignity, self-worth and identity is not recognized.

Feedback is intrinsic to the team's social structure: the coach is recording the swimmer's lap times and giving her tips on improving her performance, her teammates are encouraging her, and so on. If her performance is not her best effort, she will likely receive negative feedback.

The point is that there is a wealth of social connections and consequences to her training. These social ties may profoundly influence her training and the sacrifices she is willing to make to train so diligently, and her efforts may profoundly impact members of many groups—her family, her team and her school. The structure of her training serves an explicit social purpose as well as a personal one.

Most importantly, she understands that others are depending on her: she is needed, and her best efforts are highly valued. Her sense of dignity, self-worth and identity come from being a valued contributing member of the team. Losing a competition may hurt her pride, but the core source of her self-worth is her contributions to the team. What would wound her is feeling that she let her teammates down, that she could have performed better.

These *social elements of duty, obligation, responsibility and sacrifice* differentiate the social aspects of the two swimmers' activities. The leisurely swimmer could decide not to go to the pool and no one would feel let down. She might privately chide herself for being lazy, but she doesn't belong to a group that depends on her *sustained effort* yielding positive results.

The competitive swimmer, in contrast, has a duty as a team member to train hard and try her best to win her races. In joining the team, she accepted the responsibility to train hard *for the benefit of the team*. Though it may be unstated, she also accepted the obligation to follow the coach's instructions and encourage her teammates.

These social obligations are core to the team's functioning. If the team members feel no duty to the group and the other members, no obligation to perform well to reflect positively on the team and no responsibility to conform to the coach's program, the team falls apart: it is a team only in name. The sole pursuit of self-interest does not generate social value or serve a purpose greater than oneself.

Something else about the training swimmer's *intentional effort* is invisible to the casual observer: *the accretive nature of her work*. It takes time and consistent effort to build endurance.

This process of generating accretive results is *path-dependent*: the swimmer must advance one step at a time towards her goal. Swimming once for a few hours doesn't magically build endurance, nor does it provide enough practice time to improve the output of each stroke and kick. The swimmer cannot leap from A to Z—she must methodically advance her endurance and speed one step at a time.

The risk that all this work will come to naught is also invisible to the casual observer. The leisurely swimmer isn't wondering if her effort will be fruitless; the value of her swim is reaped in the present by the activity itself. But the swimmer in training is devoting so much time and effort to the goal that the possibility of poor results—losing all her key races—weighs heavily.

Both swimmers have *opportunity costs*: they could have chosen to do some other activity instead of swimming. The decision to go to the pool required each swimmer to relinquish other activities and goals. This foregoing of other options is the *opportunity cost* of choosing to swim.

The *sacrifice* made by each swimmer is also invisible. The leisurely swimmer may have given up the opportunity to meet friends for a meal, or the opportunity to earn additional money. The swimmer in training has far higher opportunity costs, as training requires sacrificing other options not just for one afternoon but for months or even years.

The rewards for each activity also differ. The leisurely swimmer is rewarded by the activity itself, while the training swimmer must defer the rewards of winning competitions, possibly for years.

In the financial world, we speak of *risk and return*: to reap high returns, we must accept more risk. Higher risk can lead to steep losses, so the potential cost of putting so much effort into a risky venture is high.

The training swimmer might devote years of effort to training and still lose her competitions. In seeking the high returns of winning, this swimmer had to accept the high opportunity cost and the risk that all her effort could come to naught. The high opportunity cost and risk are built into the decision to compete.

This brings us to another aspect of *sustained effort*: the productive skills, habits and values that the competitive swimmer acquires as a result of her training. If this swimmer trains hard and still loses her competitions, casual observers may consider this disappointing result a failure. Since the swimmer received no recognition for all her hard work, observers might conclude that she would have been better off investing all that time and effort in some other pursuit.

The positive results (i.e. the output) of her training, participation in the team and her competitive experiences are invisible to these observers. In their view, since she lost her competitions, all her effort was wasted. Yet in reality, the value created by her training is enormously significant, and has profound career and economic consequences. By training diligently, she acquired the enduringly productive *soft skills* of self-discipline, defining and pursuing long-term goals, monitoring her performance objectively, following her mentor's guidance, collaborating with her teammates, accepting negative feedback, and focusing on self-cultivation by advancing her skills.

In my book *Get a Job, Build a Real Career and Defy a Bewildering Economy*, I list eight essential soft skills needed to navigate the *emerging economy*—what many characterize as the *Fourth Industrial Revolution* or the *digital revolution*. These are not *hard skills* such as welding or writing software code; these are soft skills that create value in every field of endeavor.

These soft skills are *human capital*--not just the knowledge of a specific subject, but emotional, intellectual and social skills that can be productively applied to any endeavor. The social skills the training swimmer learns by participating on the team add to her *social capital*, and include the collaborative skills she gained as well as the connections to others she formed.

Such connections can have big career and economic consequences. Even if she loses competitions, her coach might recommend her for a job based on her positive contributions and perseverance, or a teammate who knows her work ethic might pass on a career-advancing opportunity.

Human and social capital have durable economic value. So even though the swimmer didn't gain the rewards of becoming a professional athlete, she still acquired human capital from the sustained effort of training, and social capital from being a team member.

There is another value to consider: the value of self-expression, of feeling acutely alive to the pleasures of swimming and competition, not just in the physical sensations of propelling oneself through the water, but of being fully oneself, of expressing something essential to one's selfhood.

Though our current system doesn't attribute much economic value to self-expression, instead viewing it as a luxury reserved for a handful of financially successful writers, artists, musicians, composers, etc., it's clear that work that aligns with one's sense of identity and purpose—

what we might summarize as our *life's work*—is qualitatively different than work performed solely out of a sense of obligation.

This alignment of identity, selfhood, mission and purpose can have career and economic consequences, as the person whose work is core to their being will continue their sustained pursuit of long-term goals even when the immediate rewards are meager. This self-generated devotion powers accretive learning that is lost to those who quit if rewards are not forthcoming early on.

Another key difference between the two swimmers is the competitive swimmer's efforts may have *a career or commercial consequence*: if she wins key races as a result of her diligent training, she may launch a professional career, her coach might get a raise, and the team might attract new commercial sponsors.

The Taxonomy and Ontology of Work

We began with the question, what is work? We are now in a position to provide some answers.

Work is not simply either/or, that is, an activity is either work or leisure; there is a complex *taxonomy of work* in which some activities have features of both work and leisure and varying levels of social value.

Work is not just an activity, it is *a state of being*; there is an *ontology of work* that encompasses an entire *internal world* of intent, purpose, goals, self-worth, identity, dignity and an awareness of being a valued contributor and *belonging,* i.e. *membership in service of a purpose greater than oneself.*

But the *ontology of work* is not only internal, for it also encompasses a complex *external network* of social connections, roles and obligations that generates far-reaching social value.

In other words, work is *a state of being that encompasses internal states and structures in the lived-in real world.* Work is an internal construct of intent, goals, identity and positive social roles and a *specific way of experiencing the world around us*: relating to people, learning skills, using tools and *expressing agency in the world*, that is, actively engaging life as a self-directed participant.

Though work encompasses an internal state of being, work is not just *in our heads; work has an external structure in the real world*, a structure that is different from that of leisure.

When we deprive people of work, we deprive them of much more than their income, which could be replaced with Universal Basic Income (UBI). We deprive them of the wealth of social and personal value that work generates. In other words, we deprive them of the opportunity to *build capital and wealth*.

I purposely chose the example of the swimmers because it wasn't muddied by money: neither swimmer was getting paid to swim, so whatever characterized the competitive swimmer's training as *work* had nothing to do with being paid to swim.

To further illuminate the taxonomy and ontology of work, let's consider another example: a person who earns money painting houses who also paints landscape canvases as an unpaid leisure activity. In addition, this person volunteers in an after-school arts program for children.

It seems simpler to explore this in the first person, so let's say I'm this painter and volunteer.

Since I'm paid to paint houses, this clearly qualifies as *work*. But as we've seen, it isn't just the payment of money that makes this *work*. My labor in a crew performing highly structured tasks has all the characteristics of work we've identified:

- Produces an output; its organizing purpose is production, not consumption
- Produces utility value and aesthetic value
- Produces readily identifiable social value to others
- Requires an intent to reach a specific production goal

- Is guided by a specific structure of working with others, performing tasks in a certain order, etc.
- Requires intentional, sustained effort
- Produces output that is measured for quality and quantity
- Generates feedback as an integral part of the organization of production
- Is needed by the crew/company and owner of the house to reach the goal
- Requires the accumulation of path-dependent skills
- Generates human and social capital
- Provides a positive social role, identity and membership in a purpose larger than oneself

We can now conclude that if an activity fulfills these functions, it is *work* even if it isn't paid. Even if I volunteer my painting labor on an unpaid crew, my activity is definitively *work*.

If an activity fulfills some of these functions, it fits somewhere into the *taxonomy of work*.

At this point, we need to introduce another key characteristic of work: *it addresses scarcity and need*. The house needs to be painted, or its metal surfaces will corrode, its wood will rot and its aesthetic value will suffer. The owner needs it painted so the property will retain its value and desirability to potential buyers.

At first glance, it may seem like there is an abundance of labor to perform this task: just about any able-bodied person can brush paint on a surface.

But the amateur's skills are not up to the task. The professional painter has learned that roughly 90% of the work is in preparing the surface for paint; the application of paint is only the last (and generally easiest) step in a multi-step process.

While one person can perform all this labor on a house, if time is a consideration then a crew of painters will get the task done much faster than one individual. This multi-person work flow requires organization, record-keeping and management. These skills are not easy to acquire, so they are intrinsically scarce.

If the owner hires an amateur, what guarantee will the owner have that the work will be completed according to high quality standards? Can the owner count on the amateur coming back to repair any defects that appear weeks after the job has been finished? Who will pay for the medical care of the amateur should he fall off a ladder and injure himself?

These considerations limit the number of individuals and organizations that can meet all these additional requirements; local painting crews who meet all these requirements are relatively *scarce* because the skills and capital needed are much higher than those available to amateurs.

The owner who is willing to accept the risks that the job will be poorly executed and have to be redone, that the painter won't repair defects, that potentially costly medical care could fall to the owner, etc., might hire an amateur. The owner who doesn't want to accept these risks will hire a painting company.

The number of painting companies with the skills, capital and financial ability to absorb all these risks is intrinsically limited, as these attributes are all costly to acquire and/or maintain. As a result, their work has *scarcity value*.

As a general rule, *profits flow to what's desirable, needed and scarce.* If a town has a relative over-supply of professional painters, the price of having a house painted will fall, as the scarcity value of painting skills has been diminished by the relative abundance of skilled painters.

Conversely, if there are only a handful of professional painting contractors in town, that *scarcity* earns a premium in the marketplace.

Note that scarcity alone does not generate a price premium; the good or service must be desired and/or needed. Let's say I'm the only worker in town who can carve ornate letters in marble. My skillset is extremely scarce. But if nobody desires or needs ornate lettering carved in marble, I can't charge a premium for my skills. Without a need to fill, a demand for this specific skill, I can't charge any more for my time than a common unskilled laborer.

Going back to our example of a painter performing three separate activities, let's consider my art activity of painting landscapes. This is a private activity, not a social one, as I paint alone. While I find fulfillment in painting landscapes, and I pursue this avocation with diligence, there is no desire or need for my canvases, as amateur landscapes are in over-supply; the town is awash in amateur paintings, and amateur painters are happy to give their output away just to clear the clutter of canvases piling up at home. But such is the over-supply, it's difficult to even give one's paintings away.

Unfortunately for me, there is essentially zero scarcity value to my output of landscape paintings. So even though my labor has many of the characteristics of work listed above, it isn't filling a need or scarcity.

It also isn't generating much social value. I work alone, and nobody depends on my production or my development of more advanced artistic skills. While I may derive a positive identity from creating art, this is an internal state, which is quite different from a *positive social role*. I am not a member serving a purpose greater than myself, nor am I contributing social value to the community.

We can now discern the outlines of the *taxonomy of work*, and shed more light on the *ontology of work*: Work fulfills the core psychological, social and economic needs of humanity.

My private activity painting landscapes may have the attributes of diligence, sustained effort, accumulation of skills, and so on, but it lacks *social and economic output*. It may fill my internal need for artistic expression, but it doesn't fill any social role or meet any economic scarcity.

It has a place in the taxonomy of work due to its output, sustained effort, etc. that differentiates it from watching TV or a leisurely activity organized around consumption, but it also has features of leisure activity.

In other words, it is not a substitute for my work on the crew painting houses. Ontologically, psychologically, socially and economically, it cannot substitute for my positive social role on a crew performing needed work.

This is why the loss of a job is so devastating. It's not just the loss of income, which may be partially replaced by unemployment insurance; it's the loss of the positive social role, of serving a purpose greater than oneself, of being needed, and contributing to a team effort that is devastating. Losing one's job isn't just an economic loss, it's a terrible psychological and social loss—and I would go further and say it is an *ontological loss*, the loss of a state of being that fulfills our core needs.

If I'm laid off from my house-painting job, I can withdraw to my little studio and paint more landscapes, but this doesn't compensate for what I've lost or dispel my grief. I miss my colleagues on the crew, our banter and jokes; I miss the satisfaction of a job well done; I miss the occasional word of praise from my supervisor or the home owner, and I miss telling friends about the projects I'm helping to complete. I miss my social network and socializing with my workplace "family."

Even if unemployment (or Universal Basic Income, should it become policy) matched my lost income dollar for dollar, that wouldn't change what troubles and saddens me: my loss of a positive social role, my no longer needed and valued, that I'm no longer contributing to something larger than myself, the loss of the opportunity to practice my craft, the loss of my social connections with my colleagues and customers, and the loss of all the other *wealth that only work generates.*

Even if I could paint landscapes, watch TV and scroll through social media for eight hours—and I can't, because they're simply not rewarding enough--these activities don't fulfill me in the same way my work did.

With this understanding, we can finally understand that the money earned by work is like the last coat of paint applied to a surface: 90% of the value is generated by other processes. Paying people to perform no work at all cannot substitute for the psychological, social, economic and yes, ontological wealth generated by work.

If you've lost your job, or seen a loved one lose a job, you know the debilitating effects of this loss. The loss manifests in many ways: difficulty sleeping, depression, loss of self-worth, the rise of mental-health and physical symptoms of distress and illness, erosion of well-being and the temptation to lash out at others.

Handing this person money actually further debilitates the unemployed person, as they realize they are now a charity case rather than a dignified and valued contributor to society.

Let's consider my third activity, volunteering in an after-school arts program for children. Here I take my interest in self-expression and painting into a classroom setting where adult volunteers create a hands-on curriculum for the children to learn how to use various mediums and materials, and practice expressing themselves through art. The school and community cannot fund the program beyond providing materials, but the school, parents and community have made it clear that they value the program and our efforts to maintain and improve it.

Once again, I'm not paid for this activity, but I'm fully engaged by the curriculum development, collaborating with other adult volunteers and parents, helping and encouraging individual children, coordinating a showing of the children's artwork, and so on.

My labor has the attributes of work (output, sustained effort, feedback, etc.) plus it has the social components that my private production of landscape paintings lacked: it generates social value to the children, their parents and families, the school and the wider community; the program's purposes is larger than myself, and *I am needed and valued*, as the number of adults with the necessary art and social skills and the willingness to devote themselves to the program in a sustained fashion is limited.

What I contribute is desirable and scarce and therefore valuable, even if my labor and the project don't generate any income.

I gain a *positive social role* by contributing to a valued community program that is widely praised.

The only aspect of work left unfilled is being paid, i.e. *financial compensation*. If funding were available, the work of the core volunteers who run the program would be paid. It isn't the value of the work that's missing—it's the funding to pay for this work.

But just as the competitive swimmer opened economic opportunities via her work ethic and contributions to the team, my unpaid role might well open doors to paid positions working with children in art programs.

But even if I don't earn a single dollar from my work in the program, I will have earned a great deal of *non-monetary wealth* for my work.

We can discern a progression here: the higher my activity advances in the taxonomy of work, the greater its value to me and to others as it fills the needs and scarcities of the community. My work in the after-school art program is rewarding in ways that my solitary efforts in my private studio could never fulfill, as there is little social value being created by my solitary production of artwork that fills no need, and little in the way of positive social role generated by solitary production of items with zero scarcity value.

While my own painting might fulfill my internal desire for self-expression, that doesn't fill the social void within me, or my need to be needed, or my desire to contribute something meaningful to a purpose larger than myself.

Scarcity and need define what's valued by the community. Leisure can pursue whatever it chooses, but the rewards of work are reserved for those who address needs and scarcities within their community.

Need as a Driving Force

The core dynamic in both leisure and work is *need*: leisure and work fulfill primal human needs. The leisure swimmer may need her private time in the pool to maintain her equilibrium in a life dominated by caring for others. The training swimmer might see membership on the team as her best chance to escape poverty.

Abraham Maslow is justly famous for his 1943 proposal of a *Hierarchy of Needs* which places the physiological needs of shelter, food, etc., at the bottom of the *Human Needs* pyramid, followed in ascending order by security/safety, love and belonging (broadly speaking, social needs), esteem needs (pride, sense of accomplishment, positive identity, respect of others, dignity) and at the apex of the pyramid, *self-actualization*, a term psychologists use to describe the flowering of purpose, meaning, creativity, morality, acceptance of others and the fulfilling of one's potential.

Maslow's hierarchy demonstrates that humans are not merely consumers of goods and services that satisfy their physiological needs. Humans need *purpose, meaning, social connections and positive social roles* as well as recreation, respite, play and leisure for self-cultivation.

Providing people with the means to satisfy their physiological needs but little else still leaves them deeply impoverished, as their higher needs will remain unfulfilled.

We've noted that *leisure and work have different structures*, as work and leisure *fill different human needs.* Our intuitive understanding of this is expressed in sayings such as *all work and no play makes Jack a dull boy.*

In an economy of rigid production roles and working hours, leisure is scarce and so we place a premium on leisure time. It's thus natural for those in highly demanding economies to assume that all human needs would best be met if we were all *paid for leisure and no longer had to work at all.* In this view, work would become optional; there would no longer be any financial need to work.

This is the foundational narrative of Universal Basic Income (UBI): once we pay everyone for leisure rather than for work, financial need vanishes and we would be free to pursue our higher needs through leisure.

But this narrative overlooks the reality that *leisure cannot fill the same needs as work because it has a completely different structure.* Indeed, if we observe people who have no work and no financial need to work, they often exhibit manifestations of profound unhappiness: a panoply of physiological symptoms and psychological ailments, low self-esteem, social dysfunction, anxiety, depression—all the signs of a *behavioral sink* resulting from a poverty of positive social roles, belonging, and sources of pride and dignity—in other words, the outputs of work.

Their higher social and esteem needs are not being met, and this generates a behavioral sink of aimlessness, dysfunction and unhappiness.

The conventional view within highly structured and demanding economies is that work is largely unfulfilling and exhausting, and Utopia is the replacement of work with 100% leisure. This is the idea of retirement: that work is replaced by leisure, and that the individual is finally free to pursue their higher needs.

But if we recall the example of the housepainter who lost his job and attempted to replace work with his solo artistic hobby, the substitution of leisure for work fails to provide the same social and esteem satisfaction he'd received from work. Since work and leisure have different structures and fill different needs, this is not a surprise; in fact, it's the only possible result, given the structural differences between work and leisure.

The housepainter regained the social and esteem fulfillment he'd lost in his (unpaid) arts education community work. Once again, it's critical to emphasize that his arts education *activity has all the characteristics of work.* Indeed, it is the program's structure of work that fulfills his social and esteem needs that his leisure hobbies left unmet.

In the conventional view, *leisure is reserved for the privileged*; the wealthy who don't have to work can dabble in the arts and enjoy life. It follows that *leisure is the key ingredient of happiness and the most important benefit of financial wealth.*

But if we examine the lives of the most educated and successful people, we find that the privilege they possess is not leisure but *the freedom to choose work they enjoy and find fulfilling*—what I earlier termed our *life's work.* The real privilege is not 100% leisure but the opportunity to pursue work that fulfills our higher needs for social connections, belonging, esteem and self-actualization.

As a general observation, people who are free to continue pursuing work they find deeply satisfying and engaging live longer, healthier lives than those who have only leisure and few opportunities to fill their higher needs.

 Although it runs counter to the conventional view, *enforced leisure is a particularly destructive form of poverty.* How do I define *enforced leisure?* Enforced leisure is a structural lack of opportunities to find our *life's work* that fulfill our higher social and esteem needs. Privilege is having the freedom to choose from a wealth of work opportunities, to mix and match meaningful work and leisure to fulfill all our needs.

Proponents of Universal Basic Income often suggest that people will use their newfound leisure to pursue artistic expression: composing poetry and music, writing novels, creating art, etc. We all understand the idea and its appeal: people would blossom creatively if only they no longer had to work.

But if we examine the lives of esteemed artists, composers and writers, a group we can broadly characterize as *creatively self-actualized*, the one common factor is a *highly structured life's work manifesting a voracious appetite for producing output.* Goethe managed a sprawling business for many years while producing a prodigious output of writing, Rachmaninoff maintained a busy schedule of performing while composing and Mahler held the demanding position of conductor while composing his major symphonies.

Whether they were paid or not for their artistic production, these *creators pursued a highly self-organized, disciplined work regime.* While leisure meets human needs for recreation and play, *the structure of leisure is incapable of yielding the same results as disciplined, sustained-effort work.* The highest human need, self-actualization, is served by activity that meets our definition of work.

While these creators may have worked on their compositions alone, they were embedded within a social structure of other artists, musicians, writers, mentors, patrons, critics, journalists, agents, galleries, salons, publishers, and so on; they were not working in solitary but within a complex *social structure that supported their work.*

The point is not the level of accomplishment they achieved; the point *is the fulfillment of social and esteem needs requires a structure that is completely different from a structure of leisure.* While creating art in isolation may fulfill a need for self-expression, it lacks the social connections and structure required to fill the higher social and esteem needs.

While the idea of freeing people to become artists is abstractly appealing, observation suggests few individuals have the requisite drive and access to a *social structure that supports their efforts* to meet their social and esteem needs via a leisurely pursuit of art. As in our example of the housepainter who pursued his landscapes painting when he no longer had to work, the leisurely pursuit of creative endeavors cannot be a replacement for the loss of social and esteem value generated by work because each has a different structure and serves different needs.

The notion that eliminating the need to work would result in universal human fulfillment and happiness is based on a profound misunderstanding of human needs and the sources of fulfillment. While humans need leisure, they also need meaningful work, and relatively few individuals exhibit the sort of self-organization that characterizes creators who generate not only artistic output but a sense of purpose, meaning and identity that has no need for social connections, belonging, etc.

In the abstract, we affirm that every human has the potential for self-actualization and creative expression. But in the real world, the self-organization and drive needed to generate a stand-alone art that fulfills all our needs is scarce. The vast majority of humans thrive not in isolation, creating a world of their own imagination, but in *social structures that fill their core social and esteem needs*—in other words, *structures of work.*

Deprived of opportunities to belong to such social work structures, humans fall into disillusionment, despair, aimlessness, anxiety, depression, and dysfunction.

If we understand the hierarchy of human needs, then we understand that a poverty of opportunities to contribute and earn dignity—that is, opportunities to fulfill our core social and esteem needs—is a poverty that a Universal Basic Income check cannot dissolve. A lack of opportunity to choose work that is fulfilling is *enforced leisure*, a form of spiritual, psychological and social impoverishment that a stipend of money can't address.

The true measure of privilege isn't just leisure—it's having the freedom and opportunity to choose meaningful work and leisure to fulfill all our needs, not just those satisfied by leisure.

Put another way, what we desire is agency—the power to control our own life's work.

The common-sense conclusion is that the entire spectrum of human needs *requires the agency to choose opportunities for work and leisure,* as each has a different structure and fills different needs.

Work doesn't just fulfill the higher social and esteem needs of individuals—*work also meets the needs of the community.* While I have focused on the inner needs of individuals in this section, *the unfilled needs of the community make work necessary and thus fulfilling to individuals.* Unnecessary work is unfulfilling, a dynamic we'll explore in the next section. What makes work necessary? *The community needs the work done to survive and thrive.*

In a market economy dominated by a strong central government that employs (directly and indirectly) a third of the work force, we assume all needs will be met by the marketplace of profit-maximizing private companies or by the public-sector government. But if we compare wealthy communities and impoverished communities, we find that neither the market nor the government serve each equally; the impoverished community has many unmet needs. The wealthy community has fewer unmet needs because its residents address the needs left unfilled by the market and the state with private wealth and volunteer labor.

The impoverished community's needs are unmet because it lacks the money to pay people to do the work that's needed. The profit-maximizing market and the state can't fill all the unmet needs of communities that lack a foundation of private capital and wealth. Clearly, we need a new mechanism that can address the unmet needs of impoverished communities. We'll explore the outlines of a *new self-funding community economy* in the book's final section.

What Makes Work Fulfilling?

While I have focused on the positives of work, we all know that much of the work people are paid to do is unfulfilling. A number of social commentators (David Graeber et al.) have written about *BS work*: work that employees know is unnecessary and therefore offers them little fulfillment. Many other dynamics can render work unfulfilling: a constantly rotating work force that deprives workers of the opportunity to form social bonds with colleagues; precarious employment; dysfunctional work places; the awareness of being a replaceable cog in an uncaring machine, and so on.

What differentiates fulfilling work from unfulfilling work?

We've already sketched out how work satisfies our social and esteem needs in ways that leisure cannot. Satisfying work has these characteristics:

-- We contribute value to our community or "tribe" (team or group).

-- Our work serves a purpose greater than ourselves.

-- Our work fills a scarcity, and makes a difference in a positive way.

-- We belong to a team and our contributions are valued by the team.

-- We make personal sacrifices to benefit the team/group.

-- Our work adds to our human and social capital; we are improving our skills and gaining social value.

-- We have the opportunity to help others in meaningful ways.

-- We are actively engaged in the group effort as a self-directed participant, i.e. we have *agency.*

Work with all eight attributes provides us with a positive social role, pride in our labor, the dignity of being useful, needed and valued, a positive self-worth, and hope for further gains in skills and social capital.

Work with none of these attributes is deeply unfulfilling. Work with just a few of these characteristics is mostly unsatisfying, and work with a majority of these characteristics is generally fulfilling.

Once again, the concept of a *taxonomy or hierarchy of work* is useful: work that has all eight attributes is at the top of the hierarchy as it meets our higher social, esteem and self-cultivation needs. Work that has few or none of these attributes is intrinsically unfulfilling because it's incapable of filling our social, esteem and self-actualization needs.

As we've noted, the privilege we should seek to make universal is not leisure alone, but *the agency to pursue both leisure and opportunities for work that has all eight of these characteristics,* i.e. *meaningful, fulfilling work.*

The Impact of High-Touch / Low-Touch on Work Fulfillment

One of the concepts that helps illuminate the *taxonomy of work* is the *high-touch, low-touch spectrum*. I used this concept in my book *Get a Job, Build a Real Career and Defy a Bewildering Economy* to explain why certain kinds of labor are more easily automated than others, and why they don't generate as much economic and social value as other types of labor.

The core concept here is that certain kinds of work offer little in the way of *social value*, i.e. the connectedness that humans crave as part of our hierarchy of needs. These kinds of work are *low-touch*, as they offer little opportunity for meaningful human contact.

Work that offer a wealth of opportunities to create social value, connectedness and cooperation is *high-touch*.

The dynamics of the high-touch low-touch spectrum help us understand what makes work fulfilling:

-- Low-touch work is particularly vulnerable to being automated, as the value created is not social. As a result, software or robotics can produce the same value as human beings, for example, a factory assembly line.

-- This lack of social value makes low-touch work more likely to be unfulfilling to employees.

IN assembly-line work, the worker has little contact with fellow employees, and essentially zero contact with customers / clients. The labor and the products have both been *commoditized* by mass production, that is, the employees are interchangeable—shifts change and the line-up of each crew changes without disrupting production— and each product is interchangeable with all the others that come off the line.

Opportunities to form meaningful bonds and generate social value are few; friendships might form during lunch breaks, but these employee bonds are often broken by re-assignments, layoffs, etc.

This kind of work is not just physically exhausting, it is a *social-value desert*, and thus inherently unfulfilling. This is why Henry Ford's first assembly line factory suffered very high rates of turnover—workers quit because the work was tedious, unrewarding and unsatisfying. This is why he had to up the rate of pay to the then unheard of wage of $5 per day—to retain workers who would otherwise quit to seek more satisfying work elsewhere. In effect, Ford had to bribe workers with higher pay to tolerate the inhuman work.

Just as low-touch production work is unfulfilling, low-touch transactions / interactions don't provide much social value to customers, either. Common examples include ordering a fast-food meal or checking out at a grocery store. Our interaction with the human being behind the counter is brief and not something valuable enough that the company can charge extra for being served by a human rather than a machine.

The employees are as interchangeable as the fast-food meals and products lining the shelves.

The vast majority of consumers accept (or may actually prefer) having a low-touch transaction served by an automated system. Rather than wait in line, many of us prefer to use the self-checkout or airport ticket kiosk. Most of us would be happy to bypass the entire time-wasting process of waiting in line to be served by a human in a low-touch transaction such as renewing our license at the Department of Motor Vehicles.

If ordering a fast-food meal is low-touch, dining at a swank bistro is high-touch. Most people would hesitate to pay swank prices for food delivered by a robot to a table in a bland booth. In other words, we're paying not just for the food but for a high-touch experience: a knowledgeable wait-person, a sommelier, an atmosphere rich with conversation, people-watching, etc.

On the factory floor, a permanently assigned team of employees who have the opportunity to work closely with clients and who have *agency*, i.e. the opportunity to become self-directed contributors to the production process, have a much more high-touch work environment than assembly-line workers with no permanent team membership, no meaningful relationship with clients and no agency (control over their work or the output of the team).

Since high-touch work produces social value, it cannot be fully replaced by software and robotics, for the *social value of human connectedness is the key output of high-touch work.*

As noted above, a product or service becomes a *commodity* when the output is interchangeable and it can be produced interchangeably in a variety of places. Technical support is a commodity, for example, as the software and/or employees providing the service are interchangeable. The Internet has greatly facilitated *digital commoditization*, as digital products and services can now be distributed at near-zero cost anywhere on the planet with an Internet or mobile phone connection.

These commoditized services are *low-touch*, as the social value created is low. The more the interaction can be standardized, the more easily it can be automated.

The net result of commoditization and automation is that many low-touch, low-skill jobs are being eliminated, and those that are left remain inherently less fulfilling due to their low social value.

Many commentators view this elimination of unfulfilling work as a boon to humanity, as workers are freed to seek more fulfilling jobs.

While we all welcome the passing of unfulfilling drudgery jobs, the mass movement of less skilled workers into higher-skill, higher-touch (and therefore more fulfilling) jobs is influenced not just by the skill level of the work force but by *cost/price*.

The Impact of Cost

As a general rule, the economic value of low-skill/ low-touch labor declines as automation eliminates these jobs as a function of simple *supply and demand*: there is a relative abundance of workers with sufficient skills to do low-touch work, and a scarcity of demand for these workers (i.e. fewer jobs).

As Immanuel Wallerstein and other socio-economists have found, the cost of labor rises with urbanization and as the work force demands more financial security: more secure old-age pensions, better healthcare and education, and so on.

This trend of higher costs for labor and labor overhead (disability, old-age pensions, healthcare, unemployment insurance, etc.) increases the incentives for employers to automate low-touch tasks as a means of reducing their production costs.

Again as a general rule, the result is that the cost of commoditized, low-touch services declines while the cost of high-skill, high-touch services rises.

Another factor driving costs for high-touch services is ever-expanding requirements for additional credentials and regulatory compliance. Many if not most high-touch services now require graduate-level diplomas and professional licenses and fees.

For example, a set of commoditized house plans can be purchased for $150 on the Internet. Hiring an architect with whom you establish a professional relationship will cost 10 times more for some limited consulting and 100 times more for a customized set of architectural plans and specifications.

Consider the future of medical care. Many observers expect software/robots to perform routine care tasks such as checking on patients to make sure they're taking their prescribed medications. This is a low-touch interaction.

While ill people won't mind interacting occasionally with a helpful robot, what they really want is a human being to stop in and express some concern for their condition. This is the high-touch connection we all want.

Low-touch is no substitute for high-touch; a hospital robot greeting us with a computer voice is not a substitute for a human doctor or nurse offering the high-touch interaction we value so highly.

As consumers, we typically won't pay extra for low-touch services provided by humans when a cheaper automated option is available: the value of the human interaction must be worth enough extra to justify a higher cost.

Employers must be sensitive to this dynamic if they want to make a profit and keep customers happy. If consumers will pay extra for a human salesperson, then salespeople will be available. But if consumers aren't willing to shoulder the higher costs of human labor, human labor in low-touch endeavors will disappear as a financial necessity.

While we won't pay extra for human labor in low-touch services, we may not be able to afford high-touch services as wages stagnate and costs of these services soar.

There are many drivers for this upward trend in the cost of delivering high-touch services such as healthcare: not just higher labor costs but the additional expenses of regulatory compliance, liability insurance, oversight, management, taxes, increased capital expenditures for new technologies and so on.

For a variety of reasons I've covered in my blog and other books, wages for the bottom 95% of households have been stagnating in the 21st century, even for highly educated workers. Add in the rising costs of living and servicing debt (student loans, mortgages, auto loans, etc.), and the amount most households can pay for high-touch services is severely limited.

Governments are also limited in how much they can pay for these services. Rapidly rising debt loads limit governments' ability to borrow more money every year to pay for increasing social welfare expenses. The net result is both private and public-sector trends are threatening the affordability and availability of the high-touch services we all value.

If these trends continue—and there is no plausible reason to expect them to reverse—high-touch services as they are currently configured may well become unaffordable for the bottom 95% of households.

We may find that the bottom 95% of households will only be able to afford services such as healthcare provided by low-touch automated systems, while the high-value, high-touch human interactions will only be affordable for the top 5%. While it's tempting to assume higher taxes can rectify this, if costs rise at a faster rate than income, higher taxes on the top 5% will not be enough to catch up with runaway costs.

All these dynamics interact in perverse ways. While the eradication of unfulfilling low-touch labor via automation is welcome in terms of freeing people to seek more fulfilling work, the higher credentialing and regulatory demands on high-touch work limit the number of workers who can meet these stiff requirements and the number of paid positions available in these fields.

Since government rely on wages for a significant share of its revenues, declines in employment and wages cause tax revenues to decline, crimping government's ability to provide increasingly unaffordable high-touch services.

The hope of many observers is that government can "tax the robots" to raise the revenues needed to provide high cost services to everyone. But these hopes are not realistic; whatever is commoditized has little pricing power and therefore generates little profit. Software and robotics are rapidly being commoditized, meaning they are interchangeable components produced in interchangeable locations.

Profits flow to what's scarce and in high demand. As software and robotics are commoditized, they become abundant. Owners of these robots cannot charge a scarcity premium, as everyone else can buy the same robotics and download the same (and often free) software.

Commoditization drives prices and profits down to a bare minimum—a dynamic Karl Marx described in the19th century. Rather than increase tax revenues, the commoditization of the tools of automation will lower profits and tax revenues.

The other hope of many—Universal Basic Income (UBI)—runs aground on the same shoals. The high cost of providing a monthly stipend to every household is not affordable to any government facing lower tax revenues and soaring debt loads, and the modest level of UBI stipends leaves recipients with little access to high-cost, high-touch services.

There is one ray of hope in this bleak snapshot of macro-trends: not all high-touch labor requires high skill levels and multiple credentials. If we designed an economy that recognizes this, we could transform both the opportunity for fulfilling work we need and deliver the high-touch services we desire.

Consider the difference between a highly trained nurse and a worker with no specialized medical skills but an ample array of social skills who visits elderly people in their homes to relieve their isolation and check that they're comfortable.

The nurse can provide high-touch, high-skill service, but at a relatively high cost. *The social-value worker* does not need much training, as the value of her visit is social, not medical. Yet absent a medical emergency, the social value of a leisurely high-touch visit exceeds the value of a brief visit by a medical professional.

If we revisit our example of the housepainter volunteering in the after-school arts program, we find the same dynamic: a high-cost, multiple-credentialed artist-educator is not only unaffordable to the school district, at the beginners' level of young students, the social value of this costly mentoring is not much greater (if at all) than the social value generated by an experienced, enthusiastic amateur: it's not the skill level of the mentor that generates the social value, it's the time, enthusiasm, caring, etc. invested in the children that generates the high-touch value for the students and the adult volunteers alike.

What if we could pay the housepainter and other volunteers for their work? In the present-day economy, this would require the government to collect more tax revenues and increase the educational-oversight bureaucracy, which would further increase costs. In our centralized hierarchical status quo, the bureaucratic tropism is to demand more credentials, more licensing, more fees, and so on, a process that only makes the program more unaffordable and thus impossible to fund.

There is another way to pay the adult volunteers for their high-value work, one that doesn't rely on government tax revenues or centralized bureaucracies. To truly understand such a radically different alternative, we must first ask a simple question with a complex answer: how do we value work?

How Do We Value Work?

Work creates output and value. But not all output earns income; much of our work is unpaid. Let's explore the relationship between creating value and earning money, i.e. paid work vs. unpaid work.

Consider a parent who takes care of her children and a neighbor's children for an afternoon. No one pays her to care for the children. Is this work, even though it's unpaid? Anyone who has watched kids knows: yes, it's work. It takes sustained effort, patience, attention, endurance—all traits of work. There is output and value: the children are guided into healthy activities while being kept safe.

Another parent cares for the same number of kids in a daycare facility, and she is paid for doing the same work. Clearly, work has no Law-of-Nature causal connection to money: some work is paid (i.e. financially compensated), while a large amount of work is unpaid.

Personal vs. Public Value of Work

Sometimes an individual puts forth effort solely for personal purposes, as in the following examples:

- A person writes an essay on the nature of work and money. No customer ordered the essay, and no government agency or private foundation funded the writing. Is it work? If you've ever composed an essay, you know the answer is yes: it takes focus, organization, effort, perseverance—all attributes of work.
- A landowner devotes considerable time and labor to restore a plot of exhausted soil to productive use by creating a preserve for native plants, insects, wild game, birds, etc. He receives no money for this work, and indeed, loses whatever income the agricultural production had yielded. Was his labor work? By any measure, his labor also qualifies as work, even though in this case it actually *decreased* his income.

Humans are naturally drawn to natural beauty. If you observe pedestrians on a street with some unkempt litter-strewn front yards and some well-maintained yards bursting with flowers, you will note that many people will stop and enjoy the flowers, while no one pauses at the weed-filled yards.

As social beings, humans are attuned to the actions of the group. A neighborhood is a group, and if you observe the actions of the owners over a period of years, you will note that when one owner repaints his house and plants flowers in his yard, nearby owners tend to make improvements on their property. Over time, this influence can trigger improvements all the way up a street. (Of course, this works in reverse as well. An abandoned house detracts from the neighborhood, and should the derelict property attract criminal squatters, the neighborhood can go downhill very quickly).

What is the output and value of the work one homeowner performs in planting and maintaining well-tended flowers that are visible to neighbors and passersby? Is the output entirely private, since the property is private? The answer is clearly no: the output and value is also *social*, for it is shared not just with the neighbors but with passersby.

Some work may appear to have no value. Suppose a person sets out to count and record the cracks in all the sidewalks around the town square. This is clearly work: there is a goal, recording of data, and a quantifiable output—there are X number of sidewalk cracks in these locations.

The fact that no one else values this data makes it unlikely anyone would pay the collector of this data for his work. Nonetheless, it is certainly work to collect and collate this data.

Clearly, work is more than *an activity that earns money. In all cases, work generates output and value.* As we've seen by all these examples:

- In some cases, identical work can be paid or unpaid, depending on circumstances that have nothing to do with the intrinsic value of the work.
- In other cases, the value of the work is not readily priced in monetary terms.
- In still other cases, the value of the work is ambiguous: it may generate some value for the person doing the work and some social value, or the value may only become apparent in the future.
- It's also possible that work's value is limited to the person performing the work, or the value accrues to Nature rather than humans.

All this raises an obvious question: Why would anyone work without being paid?

Why did the woman care for her neighbor's kids without pay? Perhaps they share their childcare duties, or perhaps the woman did the work to help the other parent through an especially trying time. Why would someone perform work to aid others, without monetary compensation? Helping others makes us feel good, a fact Adam Smith noted in his book on moral philosophy, *The Theory of Moral Sentiments* (1759).

In other words, there is *a moral quality to work as well as a social quality.*

Why would someone invest labor in a plot of land that may never return a financial gain? Perhaps for the rewards of doing something positive for the environment, or as a legacy to grandkids—there are any number of moral payoffs for restoring an ecosystem.

Why would someone work to create beauty for his neighbors and passersby to enjoy? It doesn't seem to be a moral act. Is it work for private enjoyment that happens to create social value? Or is it work specifically intended to create aesthetic value via the nurturing of beauty?

Why would someone perform the work of writing an essay with an uncertain output and return? Perhaps they want to explore a new idea or process, or perhaps they just enjoy collaborating with others. How do we calibrate the value of speculative work when the essay might have no discernable value today but might be heralded as a work of genius ten years hence?

Clearly, work cannot be reduced to strictly monetary terms; its value is intrinsically contingent and complex. There is much more to work than earning money, and much more to the value of work than whether it is paid or unpaid.

Why Is Some Work Paid and Other Work Unpaid?

Some work is paid and other work is unpaid. What differentiates work that is paid from work that earns no monetary compensation?

The basic answer is: profitable work is paid; unprofitable work is not paid.

Profit is what's left after subtracting the costs of production (labor, labor overhead such as healthcare insurance, manufacture, materials, shipping, etc.), general and accounting expenses (the overhead costs of operating the business) and capital investment required to keep the enterprise going (training of employees, replacement of outdated equipment, purchase of new technology, etc.).

No enterprise will pay for labor that doesn't generate a profit. Any enterprise that pays for unprofitable labor will soon be drained of capital and go out of business.

The State can pay people to perform unprofitable work, but since the state's revenues come from paid labor and profits, ultimately the State also depends on enterprises that are profitable because they pay taxes and have employees who pay taxes. In effect, the State can take wages from workers and profits from enterprises and use this money to pay people to perform unprofitable work, but there are limits on how much the State can take from paid workers and enterprises. If the enterprises are drained of profits, they cannot invest in future production, and they will eventually wither into unprofitability. If the State taxes payrolls to the point that workers no longer have enough disposable income to support their households, the social contract between the workers and the State breaks down.

The point here is that only a limited amount of unprofitable work can be paid in our current economic system. History suggests that States can sustainably take between a quarter and a third of all economic output (what we measure crudely with Gross Domestic Product, or GDP). Beyond those levels, private consumption and investment falter and the economy slips into a self-reinforcing recession that eventually reduces State tax revenues. If profitability and paid work are both in structural decline for systemic reasons, as I will discuss shortly, then the State's ability to pay for unprofitable work diminishes very rapidly.

There is another difference between paid and unpaid work. If someone with surplus money wants someone to perform a service for them, they have to compensate that person to perform the desired service.

This is of course the foundation of the *world's oldest profession*, prostitution, but it is also the foundation for all paid services, from auto mechanics to dog walkers to gardeners to hair cutters and so on.

The key requirement is the presence of people with surplus money to spend on services provided by others. In communities with very little money in circulation, few people have surplus money to spend on services, so instead they cut their own hair, fix their own transport, and care for their gardens themselves.

Core Conditions for Paid vs. Unpaid Work

As we have seen, any society based on a large number of people with surplus money to pay for services requires a very profitable set of enterprises that can pay people to perform profitable work and distribute some of the profits to the owners/shareholders.

If a society has such profitable enterprises, but most of the profits are distributed to a small group of owners, there won't be enough people with surplus money to support a large class of service workers. This is the classic *Plantation Economy* in which most workers are paid modest wages and the managers and owners skim the vast majority of the profits. In this type of economy, relatively few people have surplus income to spend on services.

I call this the *Neofeudal-Neocolonial Model*, as an economy that enriches the few at the expense of the many describes the feudal economies of the late Middle Ages in Europe and the classic Plantation Economy of the colonial era.

Societies with few profitable enterprises will have few paid workers and relatively little profit left to distribute to the owners. These societies cannot support a large class of service workers.

In both low-profit and Plantation Economies, there aren't enough people with surplus money to hire a large number of service workers. As a result, most of the work in these societies is unpaid.

Conversely, in cities with high concentrations of people with ample surplus income, these paid-by-profitable-enterprises people can support an enormous ecosystem of services.

If people in an economy with few paid jobs suddenly have opportunities to get paid for work they're already doing, their ability to pay for services blossoms. This surplus income from paid work then supports the expansion of a private service sector and increases the State's tax revenues, enabling the State to provide even more services. The wider the spectrum of work that is paid, the greater the surplus income available to pay for additional services, a dynamic that generates more paid work in a virtuous self-reinforcing cycle.

This may seem too obvious for comment, but it's the core connection between work, money and poverty: the way to alleviate poverty is to widen the spectrum of work that is paid, which then gives people the means to buy services that generate paid work for those providing the services.

We've seen that work is much more than earning a livelihood. Work is the engine of identity, purpose, meaning, pride in one's contributions and social value. Giving unemployed people a Universal Basic Income (UBI) stipend but no paid work may give them the means to buy the bare necessities of life, but it can't provide the wealth of connections, human and social capital, purpose, value and meaning that comes only from paid work.

Let's examine what happens when paid work disappears and is replaced with social welfare programs such as Universal Basic Income.

II. The Desertification of Life: When Work Disappears

We've covered the wealth of individual and social benefits generated by work, and briefly discussed the negative consequences to the individual when work disappears. I've expressed these negative consequences in terms of the deprivations imposed by the disappearance of work: the individual no longer has the opportunity to build human and social capital, create social value, earn self-respect and pride, derive satisfaction from meaningful work, accept responsibilities, make sacrifices on behalf of something greater than himself, or to express his selfhood through work.

But the disappearance of work is more than a loss of opportunity. It is *a desertification of identity, spirit and soul.* The person with no work, and no hope of work, lives in a sea of humiliation. Others have purpose, a meaningful role, the respect of others and a source of self-worth and pride, while the person with no work is acutely aware of others' condescension. This wounded pride and lack of self-worth savages the workless person and those closest to him/her.

Addiction is a complex phenomenon, but it is no coincidence that addictive behavior soars in areas where work has disappeared. When there is no other reason to get up in the morning, feeding an addiction serves as a purpose in life. Drugs numb the humiliation, the pain, the hopelessness and the degradation of workless lives.

The locale doesn't matter, and neither does the gender, ethnicity, faith or political affinity of those whose work has disappeared. When work disappears, the same self-destructive behaviors and social dysfunctions arise in both urban and rural environments.

When work disappears, the destruction is not limited to the identity and spirit of the workless individuals; the built landscape is scarred and the social fabric is shredded. No wonder visitors to places where work has disappeared describe "a war zone:" the buildings look bombed out, and the survivors are shell-shocked. The community and its inhabitants have suffered *social defeat*.

While *social defeat* is generally defined as the result of losing a conflict—a definition drawn from studies of colonies of rodents—I use the term to describe the mutually reinforcing dysfunctions we observe in communities that have been stripped of paid work: alienation, apathy, epidemics of drug use, random violence, and so on. In effect, people stripped of the opportunity for paid work have lost a Darwinian conflict: those on top of the wealth-power pyramid have well-paid work and status, those who lost do not.

While the State provides social welfare (unemployment, disability, food stamps, etc. in the U.S.), the sharp decline in disposable income resulting from the disappearance of paid work soon hollows out local commerce, as few have money for much beyond essentials. And as small businesses close, the decline is self-reinforcing: every enterprise that shuts down means more people have lost their livelihood, and then there is even less money circulating in the ravaged local economy.

The only businesses with the means to pay rent are large corporations, so locally-owned businesses disappear along with work, leaving a few corporate-owned outlets and a handful of thrift/jumble shops, predatory "payday" lenders and perhaps a liquor store or marijuana dispensary to meet the demand for legal self-medication.

Landlords, unable to attract tenants, give up maintaining their buildings, and the local government lacks the tax revenues or borrowing capacity to buy up the decrepit building stock and redevelop it.

The connections tying paid work and commerce to social organizations such as churches, schools and civic groups fray and break. Organizations that serve the community become overwhelmed, and are thrust into a survival mode of struggling to maintain minimal services.

Government, drained of the tax revenues lost when paid work and commerce both dried up, attempts to maintain social order and the bare-bones civic services of education, streetlights, etc.

Social spaces—public and private venues for social gatherings, performances, farmer's markets, etc. —become grim and uninviting, or even dangerous. This process of social decline is as self-reinforcing as the loss of paid work and the decline of commerce: as public events disappear, so do all the ties such events nurtured.

The disappearance of paid work triggers a self-reinforcing process of *social defeat*: as commerce retreats, tax revenues dry up, affecting schools; property values decline, exacerbating the drop in tax revenues; the few who try to start a new enterprise are defeated by rigid, self-serving political systems left over from a more prosperous time, and the blight spreads across the physical and social landscape.

Observers can usually detect a Pareto Distribution in this self-reinforcing malaise, i.e. when 20% of the workforce has lost their jobs, there is an outsized impact on the remaining 80%.

Over time, the *collective memory of how the community once functioned* fades and is eventually lost. Leaders retire, old-timers die and the ambitious move away in search of better opportunities. This is a devastating loss of *human and social capital*: once the knowledge of how to start and operate an enterprise is lost, commerce becomes an alien territory. The knowledge of how to gather the community to accomplish projects is lost, crippling the self-help strategies preached by outsiders.

Though the government might fund job-training programs, once the collective memory of work is lost, the job training is like a handful of water tossed on a parched landscape: the trainees have no collective experience of productive work habits to draw upon.

Institutions lose the ability to perform community-service task they once accomplished routinely. Banks stop loaning to new businesses (assuming any banks are left); churches give up hosting the annual bazaar, the Chamber of Commerce abandons the annual parade, and so on.

This social and physical decline then spreads as local government is pressured to close under-utilized post offices, schools and parks. These closures make the community even less appealing to potential residents, investors and employers.

The number of stakeholders with the means and will to launch a new cycle of investment that might lead to the renewal of work dwindles: when the plant closes, more than the jobs are lost. The company had a stake in the community, and its engagement and funding supported a web of connections and activities.

Under this spreading cloud of hopelessness, the number of people willing to invest in maintaining the community's standards declines. Fruit trees are cut down as "too much bother," abandoned houses are burned down for amusement or occupied by destructive squatters, and the ugliness seeps into every nook and cranny of the landscape.

This is the *desertification not just of opportunities for work but of life*. The desertification of opportunities for work triggers the *desertification of the entire community*: the built environment, the natural and social landscapes and the inner life of those abandoned when paid work disappears.

Our Failed Coping Mechanisms and the Denial of Loss

We are all aware that technological change is accelerating, and that this process is transforming the economies and societies of the world in unpredictable ways. Though the economic and convenience benefits are heralded daily in the mainstream media, the destruction of previously stable ways of living receives much less attention.

Technology is deaf and blind to the carnage it leaves in its wake; in our current system, it's viewed as a force of Nature much like a giant, never-ending tornado that roams the planet, tearing up economies, societies and cultures and leaving the survivors to sort through the wreckage.

Our institutional and individual coping mechanisms are both from another era—an era of abundant paid work. The institutional response is always "here's some money to tide you over until you find another job, and if you're having trouble, here's some job training to prepare you for a career change."

Individually, our healthcare and mental health systems rely on medications and optimism. Those devastated by the loss of work may at best receive a few counseling sessions paid by insurance, a prescription for anti-anxiety and anti-depression medications, and a list of websites offering advice on maintaining a positive attitude. Go get 'em, Tiger!

The inadequacy—or perhaps we should say the *depravity*-- of these coping mechanisms is painfully obvious. As paid work becomes scarce, job training has little effect on the opportunities for paid work.

This reliance on medications and a few spurts of counseling addressed the old need to help the newly jobless get through brief periods of unemployment. These coping mechanisms no longer fit the economic and social realities of the world we inhabit.

Many observers believe the economy will always generate more new jobs than it destroys with technological advances such as automation. In this mindset, all that's needed is to retrain the unemployed to fill the new jobs being created.

But there is little evidence for this belief. The vast majority of the jobs created in the 21st century in the U.S. are low-skilled "old economy" jobs such as waiter and bartenders, typically poorly paid, often part-time and contingent on a constantly shifting work schedule. The total percentage of the work force employed in high-tech sectors has barely budged.

In effect, mainstream commentators are in denial about the erosion of secure paid work and opportunities for finding secure paid work, and the devastating impact this structural erosion is having on people, families and communities.

The conventional solutions—more education, more diplomas, more credentialing—have only created an abundance of credentials, not an abundance of jobs. As I have noted before, issuing 100,000 masters degrees in chemistry doesn't automatically generate 100,000 new jobs. Having workers with advanced degrees is only one piece of the complicated dynamics of creating a profitable job.

Supporters of Universal Basic Income (UBI) promote the idea that recipients of UBI will be free to start enterprises or take whatever jobs they desire. This idealized gloss ignores the same dynamic described above: paid work doesn't arise by magic simply because people are willing to work or have a new credential in hand, nor can a community stripped of capital and the collective memory of entrepreneurship magically generate new enterprises in a desert of social and financial capital.

This systemic failure to grasp the fundamentals of creating paid work suggests that the fields of psychology, technology and economics don't really talk to each other. The field of economics thrills to the accelerating pace of technological change; this drives the economic narratives of *creative destruction* and improving productivity, and ignores the losses described above. The typical view of economists is that creative destruction is tough at first, but everyone prospers in the end. That this is magical thinking is never mentioned publicly.

Conventional psychology is equally blind to the tremendous losses inflicted on individuals and communities by this structural acceleration of disruptive change--what Marx described as *everything solid melts into air*. For Marx, modern capitalism melted everything into air by its very nature. It wasn't a feature of capitalism that could be eliminated or even limited. As the *mode of production* changed, it upended everything from work to family to the built environment around us.

As the tornado sweeps through, destroying everything we cherish, the fields of psychology and psychiatry are trained to respond to individuals' anxiety and depression in isolation—here are coping mechanisms you can learn, here are medications you can take, etc. The fields that are tasked with maintaining our mental health seem blind to the systemic cause of so much of our anxiety, depression and sense of loss.

The notion that we need time and space to mourn what we've lost in all this accelerating insecurity and disorientation is apparently alien to modern cultures. There is no process or cultural space for mourning lost careers, lost social roles, lost identities, lost communities, lost friends, lost relationships; these are considered individual losses rather than the inevitable output of the system we are part of. Such mourning is verboten, perhaps because the act of recognizing our losses calls into question the insecurity and sanity-draining stresses of our way of life. No mourning is allowed for the disruption of everything we cherished most.

The American ideal is an optimism that is dismissive of losses and mourning for what has been sacrificed or destroyed. "It is what it is" is now our only balm; resignation, a frozen grin of conjured optimism and a numbing of all the pain with medication. Perhaps we're terrified of recognizing our losses to accelerating change--a disorienting disintegration that never seems to increase our security or connectedness with others.

The media cheerleaders of these accelerating changes promote social media and Universal Basic Income (UBI) as the substitutes for the sense of belonging, of paid work that gave us pride and satisfaction, of a sense of place that included a collective memory of how a community functions, and relationships that aren't contingent on the next round of layoffs.

The Loss of Social Roles and Meaning

Henry Ford famously raised the wages of his factory workers to the then-extraordinary rate of $5 per day. The publicly-touted reason was so the workers could afford to buy one of the autos they were manufacturing.

The real reason is quite different. Workers hated the mind-numbing repetition and physically exhausting work in the factory so much that they quit in droves. Turnover was very high. Men would be hired, experience the realities of the actual work environment, and then quit. So Henry Ford had to double the wage to bribe workers to endure the deadening work for the sake of higher disposable income.

Karl Marx described the alienation of the worker from the product of his/her labor as follows: the worker no longer had a stake in the output, because the output was owned by the factory owner. The worker owned nothing but his/her weekly wage. The self-employed craft worker, in contrast, owned his/her output and could build a stake in the local economy.

But this is not the sum total of alienation. Even if the work was deadening and the worker had no stake in the product, at least he/she had a *positive social role* in society, a positive standing among peers and a positive self-definition.

"I work at the Ford plant." Having paid work is a positive role; everyone admires the worker for pulling their own weight and contributing to society with their labor and taxes.

Everyone wants a positive role within their peer groups of fellow employees, church/temple members, neighbors, friends and extended family. Even if the worker loathes the job, having a job in the plant offers him/her a positive role that peers immediately understand; no explanation is required.

All humans want a positive self-image and positive self-definition of their identity. Paid work provides that positive self-definition, even if the work is low status or poorly paid. One can say: "I make my own money, I am helping to support my family, I don't let my fellow employees down by slacking, and I show up on time no matter how much I hate this job. I am a good worker and stand ready to help my fellow employees."

A job provides dignity, self-worth, purpose, goals, the *agency* (i.e. independence of action) provided by earning money that can be spent in all sorts of ways, and pride—"yes, this job is hard, boring and tiring, but I manage to hold up my end."

Though the work itself may be demeaning, the positive social roles and self-respect that come with paid work provide *meaning*. Paid work provides three human essentials:

1. a positive social role,
2. a positive role amongst peers, and
3. a source of purpose, self-respect and pride.

These three essentials are the foundation of human happiness and positive social networks.

The Filipina maids of wealthy Hong Kong families offer a striking example of this. A sociology study found that the maids, who work six days a week for low wages in often-demeaning situations, gathered in a park on their one day off (Sunday). There they find the warmth of friendship, camaraderie and the emotional support of peers.

The maids do this demeaning work for low pay to support their families back home in the Philippines. Their work has purpose, and this provides the dignity, self-worth and self-respect that the work itself does not provide. The researchers expected to find much misery amongst the maids and much happiness among their wealthy employers, but it turned out the opposite was true. Since the maids had those three essentials listed above, they were markedly happier than their wealthy employers, who were characterized by depression, unhappiness and thoughts of suicide.

A 2017 article in the *Harvard Business Review* summarized the impact of joblessness that I've attempted to describe here: *Does Work Make You Happy? Evidence from the World Happiness Report:*

"One of the most robust findings in the economics of happiness is that unemployment is destructive to people's wellbeing. We find this is true

around the world. The employed evaluate the quality of their lives much more highly on average as compared to the unemployed. Individuals who are unemployed also report around 30 percent more negative emotional experiences in their day-to-day lives.

The importance of having a job extends far beyond the salary attached to it. A large stream of research has shown that the non-monetary aspects of employment are also key drivers of people's wellbeing. Social status, social relations, daily structure, and goals all exert a strong influence on people's happiness.

Not only are the unemployed generally unhappier than those in work, we find in our analyses that people generally do not adapt over time to becoming unemployed. More than this, spells of unemployment also seem to have a scarring effect on people's wellbeing, even after they have regained employment."

The experience of joblessness can be devastating to the individual in question, but it also affects those around them. Family and friends of the unemployed are typically affected, of course, but the spillover effects go even further. High levels of unemployment typically heighten people's sense of job insecurity, and negatively affect the happiness even of those who are still in employment.

Money alone does not provide a positive social role, a positive role amongst peers, or a source of purpose, self-respect and pride. Instead, it appears that purposeful work and a strong social network of supportive peers and friends are the things that generate the foundation of human happiness.

The Emptiness of Consumerism

When a person loses their job, they don't just lose the income – as we've seen, they also lose a source of the three essentials for human fulfillment and happiness.

This is the fundamental flaw of Universal Basic Income (UBI): the idea that as automation replaces human labor, the solution is to pay every household a basic income, with no strings attached. The tragic fallacy of this well-meaning notion is that giving everyone free money but no source of purpose, positive social roles, self-respect and pride dooms recipients to the Hell of social defeat.

This assumption is rooted in the belief that being a consumer is the source of meaning and happiness in the modern era: if people have money to spend, and the leisure to consume, they have the foundation of human happiness.

But consumerism is not a foundation of human well-being or happiness. Instead, it is a source of anxiety (because others can consume more and better things than I can) and an erosion of identity, as the only self that exists in consumerism is the identity projected by brand identifiers and signifiers: what you are wearing, where you're seen dining, etc.

Christopher Lasch explained these dynamics in his landmark book *The Culture of Narcissism: American Life in an Age of Diminishing Expectations*. Lasch identified the rise of consumerism as the source of a culture of narcissism. For Lasch, the relentless commoditization of life disrupted the natural social relations of family, social reciprocity and the workplace, depriving individuals of these sources of meaning and replacing them with an empty consumerism that worshipped brands and celebrity.

The marketplace's commoditization of everyday life--both parents working all day for corporations so they could afford childcare, for example--creates two alienating dynamics: a narcissistic, entitled personality crippled by a fragile sense of self that seeks solace in consumerist identifiers (wearing the right brands, etc.), and a therapeutic mindset that sees alienation not as the consequence of commoditization but as individual issues to be addressed with self-help and pop psychology.

In Lasch's view, both of these dynamics ignore the loss of authenticity that results from the commoditization not just of production but of every aspect of everyday life.

Lasch's social analysis is an extension of Marx's original insight into the alienating dynamics of commoditized wage-work, in which workers and their work were both interchangeable.

Personal gratification is the driver of narcissism and consumerism, which are two sides of the same coin. On the one hand, consumerist marketing glorifies the *projected self* as the *true self*, encouraging self-absorption even as it erodes authentic identity, self-esteem and resilience, all of which enable emotional growth, the essential characteristic of adulthood. An obsession with personal gratification generates self-absorption, fragile self-esteem and an identity that is anxiously dependent on consumerist signifiers to win the approval of others.

Proponents of Universal Basic Income (UBI) routinely claim recipients will be free to take whatever work they want, create art, start businesses, etc. But beneath this feel-good fantasy, the reality is that UBI is understood as a substitute for paid work. UBI proponents are so ensnared in the commoditized consumerist ethos that they do not even recognize the inescapably destructive impact that giving everyone money but no positive social roles, purpose or opportunities for meaningful, fulfilling work will have on human happiness. As I have explained, what this will deliver is a Hell of dependency, anxiety, social defeat and a debilitating *permanent adolescence* of insecurity and narcissism.

The Loss of Local Production and Social Cohesion

The implicit foundation of Universal Basic Income is that *consumption and leisure* are ideal substitutes for *production*, which will be automated on a global scale by the magic forces of the marketplace. The consequences of these implicit assumptions are ignored by advocates of UBI.

Marx's term for a civilization's economy, society and culture, *Mode of Production,* is based on the understanding that human life and society are organized around *production*, not consumption. (Pre-agriculture hunter-gatherers actively harvest the production of the local environment, a process that's not to be confused with passive consumption of goods produced by distant corporations.)

Production requires social cooperation, and is thus the source of *social cohesion*, the glue that binds groups, communities and societies together. Consumption does not require social cooperation; rather, it is an atomizing process of individuals seeking to bolster their fragile consumption-dependent social status.

The supporters of Universal Basic Income make a series of implicit assumptions about the process of production, apparently with little or no awareness of their acceptance of the current *Mode of Production*: a globalized, centralized, corporate-state marketplace in which everything has been commoditized: finance, resources, labor, automation, the tools of political influence, and so on.

Judging by the many essays in favor of UBI, this globalized *Mode of Production* is a complete mystery to the vast majority of UBI supporters, who assume products will magically be produced by global corporations' robots somewhere on the planet (where doesn't matter to consumers) and shipped to consumers ready to spend their UBI stipend.

The advocates of UBI implicitly assume that this neoliberal, neocolonial, neofeudal mode of production is 1) *wonderful because it effortlessly produces goods and services without requiring any human labor;* 2) *the only possible Mode of Production* and 3) *endlessly sustainable.* These assumptions are profoundly false, for reasons that I have elaborated in my previous books.

In summary, this neoliberal, neocolonial, neofeudal Mode of Production is unsustainable, exploitive and immensely destructive to the planet and everyone caught up in it. By destroying local production, this system also destroys social cohesion (i.e. social capital). By substituting consumption for production, this system destroys social cooperation in favor of atomized, narcissistic consumers trapped in permanent adolescence. Stripped of opportunities for the positive social roles created by production, individuals suffer all the ills of social defeat.

In a fully commoditized global economy, local production cannot compete with distant global concentrations of capital. And so the localized ecosystem of producers and small business owners are plowed under by the Walmarts of the world, and then even the local Walmart closes.

The Guardian newspaper (United Kingdom) published a painfully insightful report in July 2017, *What Happened When Walmart Left* McDowell County, West Virginia. Once local production was plowed under by globalized production and distribution, as epitomized by Walmart, a number of destructive dynamics were unleashed.

Social spaces were in effect commercialized. With Main Street abandoned, the local Commons—the town square or equivalent—were also deserted. The local Walmart—a privately owned outpost of a global corporate power with one goal, maximizing profit—became the primary social space in the community: people went to Walmart to see their friends and people-watch, while away time walking the aisles, etc. When the Walmart store closed, the community lost not just a primary source of paid work but its social space.

The core dynamic of local production is that it is responsive to local scarcities and needs. A commoditized, globalized Mode of Production also *commoditizes demand*: the local community is slowly starved of everything that isn't supplied by global capital—most importantly, the social cohesion that is generated by local production.

Once the skills and capital needed for local production are lost, there is no way to recover them without creating a new *Mode of Production* that not only funds local production but incentivizes it.

The problem with Universal Basic Income is that it is blind to these fundamentally destructive dynamics of commoditized production and consumption. As a result, it is also blind to the systemic need for an entirely new Mode of Production based on *DeGrowth* (consuming less of everything, valuing social capital above financial capital) and relocalizing production to rebuild social capital and cohesion.

Universal Basic Income establishes the right goal—financial and material security—but it leaves all the higher human needs unaddressed. As I will explain in detail in the next section, *UBI has the right goal but is the wrong mechanism* for two reasons—it is a flawed social construct based on a flawed Mode of Production, and it fails to address humanity's higher needs for purpose, social cohesion, meaningful work and positive social roles.

Can't we do better than guarantee the material basics of survival? Why can't we guarantee what the elite considers its birthright—not just material survival but access to positive social roles, meaningful work and opportunities to build capital?

To accomplish this, we need a new social construct for money and work, which I will sketch in the last section of this book. (This new social construct is the subject of my previous book *A Radically Beneficial World: Automation, Technology and Creating Jobs for All.*)

To design social constructs of work and money that actually achieve the goal of providing security for all, we must first complete a radical critique of the widely proposed solution, Universal Basic Income.

III. The Fantasy World of Universal Basic Income

Proponents of Universal Basic Income (UBI) have embraced UBI as the solution to the erosion of jobs by automation and the resulting insecurity for those exposed to a loss of livelihood. UBI enthusiasts believe that having to work for a living keeps people from expressing their artistic/creative urges, and the leisure enabled by UBI will make people happy and fulfilled because they will have the time and freedom to do anything they want.

Supporters believe those freed from the demands of paid work will use their newfound freedom to start new entrepreneurial businesses because they no longer have to risk their livelihoods; they can afford to fail, as their monthly income is guaranteed.

Enthusiasts also believe recipients of UBI will take jobs to earn more income, since they won't lose the UBI benefit by earning more income. (Assuming the tax structure remains progressive, those earning more income will however pay higher tax rates on their earned income.)

All of this sounds idyllic. But does it align with what we've learned actually makes people happy and fulfilled? Does it align with the financial and economic realities of our globalized, commoditized, credit and growth-dependent economy?

I share the same goal of providing systemic security for all. But we have to separate good intentions from false assumptions and destructive policies. Good intentions appeal to the idealistic and ease the guilt of elites, but they aren't substitutes for an in-depth analysis of the 95% of the UBI iceberg that's below the idealized surface.

Let's first describe the main tenets of UBI.

The Core Tenets of Universal Basic Income

Though there are many variations of Universal Basic Income, the explicit core tenets are:

1. Monthly cash payments are distributed to every adult: the benefit is universal and is paid regardless of the individual's wealth, income, willingness to take a job or financial need. In other words, there are no strings attached; every adult receives the same monthly payment, rich and poor alike.
2. The purpose of UBI is to eliminate material poverty, so the payment must be sufficient to fund each recipients' food, shelter and other material needs—the bottom layer of Maslow's hierarchy of needs. In other words, the goal is to provide universal material security.

The implicit (i.e. unstated but assumed) core tenets are:

1. Automation and robots will replace most human labor, resulting in permanent unemployment for tens of millions of people.
2. The leisure created by UBI will be a great boon to those freed from work. Those freed from the burdens of work will flower, creating art and starting new enterprises.
3. UBI will be politically popular because it is universal: since everyone will receive the entitlement, the majority of people will support UBI.
4. The secondary goal of UBI is to reduce wealth and income inequality by taxing the wealthy and redistributing this tax revenue to every adult.
5. Progressive taxation will effectively claw back UBI benefits paid to the wealthy.
6. Automation and robots are highly profitable, and the immense costs of UBI will be paid by taxing robots and the corporations that own them.

The goals of UBI—providing material security for all, reducing wealth and income inequality and the freeing of the unemployed from the insecurities of the current Mode of Production—are worthy and admirable. But Universal Basic Income's (UBI) core assumptions are fatally flawed, and its enthusiasts ignore the practicalities because they sabotage the entire concept.

If we consider the centrality of work to human happiness and fulfillment, and the soul-crushing poverty imposed by *forced leisure*, we see that while Universal Basic Income has a good goal—universal material security—it can't fulfill that goal because its structure is fatally flawed, not just practically but conceptually. Even worse, UBI leaves all the other human needs above the basic material needs unmet.

The Three Arguments in Favor of UBI

The arguments in favor of Universal Basic Income distill down to three fundamental propositions:

Advocating UBI is the moral high ground. UBI is a highly moral policy, as it offers universal security and leisure—the two things humans want most.

UBI is necessary because there's no other alternative way to provide for the permanently unemployed. Since robots (or more broadly, automation) will perform most of the work currently done by humans, what other substitute for market-based paid work is there?

UBI is financially and economically practical. Since robots will be doing the profitable work previously performed by humans, the robots will generate plentiful profits, which can be taxed to fund UBI. Furthermore, the economic activity (consumption) generated by UBI will be so great that taxing this activity will generate enough taxes to fund UBI. In other words, UBI will be essentially self-funding.

Each of these arguments is based on a number of implicit assumptions. If we make these assumptions explicit and examine them closely, a much darker and more complex understanding of UBI emerges.

It turns out that UBI is the exact opposite of what its proponents claim: it is morally bankrupt and unjust; it is not the only alternative, and not only it is financially and economically impractical, it is deeply destructive—not just to those relegated to the bottom of the wealth-power pyramid, but to the planet we inhabit.

The Implicit Assumption: The Elite Class is Superior

We can cut to the heart of the elitist assumptions underpinning UBI by asking of its advocates: would you be happy with a subsistence stipend and near-zero prospects for acquiring a career and capital? Would you be happy to spend your leisure writing poetry, as proponents of UBI foresee recipients doing with their abundance of free time?

Wait a minute, the UBI advocate protests; *UBI isn't for people like me.* It's for everyone who isn't capable of doing all the things I can do.

This gets us close to the uncomfortable truth: UBI advocates implicitly understand they are members of a self-serving elitist class.

This elite class is pleased to define itself as merit-based: *we are morally and intellectually superior, and thus our privileges are deserved.*

Their moral and intellectual superiority grants the elitist class members access to what's scarce: fulfilling careers, positive social roles and opportunities to build capital/wealth.

As for the 90% who are denied access to these scarcities: they lost the Darwinian battle for membership in the elite class, and so they're fortunate to get the elites' condescending solution, UBI: you should be grateful that we're generously offering you just enough crumbs to scrape by. Oh, and though the poetry you compose will be mostly bad (it's a pity you didn't have what it takes to attain our educational and cultural sophistication), a few gems might emerge; we'll let you know from the glorious heights of our own lofty accomplishments.

Once we understand the implicit elitist class structure of UBI, we understand that it is morally bankrupt, for it perpetuates a corrupt, unjust and unsustainable financial-political hierarchy. Rather than advance those displaced by automation, UBI institutionalizes a two-tier economy of haves and have-nots, formalizing a permanent underclass under the do-gooder guise of UBI.

What Do the Wealthy Have That the Poor Don't Have?

Stripped of idealist cant, UBI is actually a system that ring-fences what's desirable and scarce—*opportunities for positive social roles, fulfilling careers and acquiring capital/wealth*—for the elite class at the top of the wealth-power pyramid and relegates everyone else to a misery-inducing poverty that's presented, in perfectly Orwellian fashion, as an idyllic paradise.

This isn't what the idealistic supporters of UBI want to hear, but it's the truth. UBI absolves the elites of their guilt for securing the privileges of *agency, opportunity and capital* for themselves.

The cold political reality is that denying the non-elites opportunities to obtain the material basics would trigger political disorder, something the elite class atop the wealth-power pyramid fears. So the implicit political goal of UBI is to distribute just enough of the material basics so the bottom 90% have no motivation to rise up and demand systemic reorganization.

The great irony of UBI is that the distribution of material security sounds so noble, but it's actually crassly political in purpose and cruel in that it keeps non-elites alive but does nothing to meet their higher needs for dignity, pride, purpose, meaning, positive social roles and all the other forms of wealth provided by meaningful work.

A truly beneficial system would guarantee opportunities for positive social roles and building capital, not just enough cash to scrape by. A truly beneficial system would guarantee universal opportunities for *high-touch* paid work to all—in other words, the opportunity to acquire wealth in all its forms.

What we need is a system that offers everyone what the elites have: not just material security, but opportunities for agency, the building of capital and opportunities for fulfilling careers.

One way to understand this is to ask: *what do the wealthy have that the poor don't have?*

On a superficial level, we can describe all the luxuries that the wealthy can afford that the poor cannot: mansions, exotic sports cars, caviar for breakfast and so on. In a society defined by excessive consumerism, the list of consumerist luxuries available to the wealthy is practically endless.

Isn't there more to wealth than this superficial layer of consumerist signifiers of status? Beyond access to luxury consumer goods, *what do the wealthy have that the poor don't have?*

The answer is *wealth.* But what is wealth?

The superficial answer is *lots of money.* Anyone with a vault of cash is wealthy. The classic example is a winner of a multi-millionaire-dollar lottery: the winner is instantly wealthy.

But if we dig a bit deeper, we ask: what's the source of the wealthy elites' money?

The answer is *productive assets,* i.e. assets that generate income such as commercial buildings, stocks and bonds. The top 10% of American households own over 75% of all these assets, the top 5% own roughly 65% and the top sliver—one half of one percent—own a third of these assets.

If there is anything that separates the wealthy from non-elites, it's ownership of productive assets—not jewels and sports cars, but assets that produce income. If you own a diamond necklace, it just sits there. If you own a bond, it produces income every month that you can then spend or invest.

But how did they get these productive assets? Many elites inherit their wealth from their parents. But many acquire these assets on their own. How did they do it?

The answer is *capital.* Capital is of course the root of *capitalism* (private enterprise), but it's also the root of socialism, which is simply *public ownership of capital.*

What exactly is capital? Most people understand money is a form of capital, because cash earns interest, and that factories, mines, lumber mills and oil wells are tangible forms of capital.

But many other forms of capital are intangible, such as *intellectual capital* (knowledge, experience and skills, also known as *human capital*) and *social capital* (productive networks of collaborators, mentors, customers, suppliers, etc.). Author Peter Drucker (among others) argues that as our economy is *knowledge-based*, the most valuable form of capital isn't cash or tangible capital, it's human capital—being able to create value with knowledge and skills.

In Section Two of my book *Get a Job, Build a Real Career and Defy a Bewildering Economy*, I describe the five essential forms of non-financial capital: human and social capital, *cultural and symbolic capital*, and *infrastructure capital*. Together these form the *infrastructure of opportunity*. Without all five forms of capital working together, opportunity is extremely limited.

To better understand *cultural and symbolic capital*, let's consider an example of a young fellow who grew up in a family network of entrepreneurs. He understands the *culture of entrepreneurship*: the necessity of taking risks, of working long hours, of the family working together in the enterprise, of cultivating clients and customers, of constantly developing new markets and products, of keeping tabs on trends and competitors, and so on.

He understands how to make use of the *symbolic capital* of vendor credit, purchase orders, and the like.

He also understands how to make use of the *entrepreneurial infrastructure* around him: the lenders, vendors, suppliers, trucking and air freight companies, local government agencies, media outlets and other networks that underpin any entrepreneurial project.

If he faces a thorny problem, he can consult more experienced family members; in other words, he also has abundant *social capital*.

Now compare this fellow to a person of equal age, intelligence and formal education who has no knowledge or experience of the many forms of symbolic capital embedded in a culture of entrepreneurship. As for the infrastructure of entrepreneurship—it's largely invisible to him.

Let's say neither person has any cash or tangible capital—neither owns any land, a workshop, etc. Both have an idea for a new enterprise.

Which one has the greater opportunity to create a livelihood that will not only generate income and capital but that will be fulfilling, i.e. meeting his higher needs? Which one has the greater opportunity not just to succeed in the conventional definition (i.e. making money) *but of having fun doing so?*

I think we all recognize the immense advantages possessed by the young fellow with the *wealth of intangible capital* (social, cultural, symbolic and infrastructural). This intangible wealth enables him to start a business without much cash and nurture it to success—and have a tremendously fulfilling time doing so--*even if the enterprise fails.* For the culture of entrepreneurship is grounded on the acceptance of failure, as failure is the greatest teacher: *fail often, fail fast.*

If we scrape away the superficialities of diamond necklaces and yachts, what the wealthy have that the poor don't have is access to credit (financial capital) and all five forms of intangible capital. With this capital in hand, the *wealthy have opportunities the poor do not.* The wealthy have access to an *infrastructure of opportunity* that the poor do not.

As Erik Brynjolfsson, Andrew McAfee, and Michael Spence observe in their 2014 article *New World Order: Labor, Capital, and Ideas in the Power Law Economy,* ordinary financial capital and labor have very little scarcity value; value and profits flow to what's scarce and in high demand. As they explain:

"Fortune will instead favor a third group: those who can innovate and create new products, services, and business models.

So in the future, ideas will be the real scarce inputs in the world -- scarcer than both labor and capital -- and the few who provide good ideas will reap huge rewards."

Consider what billionaires such as Oprah Winfrey, Bill Gates and Warren Buffet do with their time. They obviously don't need to work for a living; they could sit in a vault running their fingers through jewels, gold coins and precious objects all day, or while away their time on their private yacht.

But they don't: they choose to work, because *work is what's rewarding fulfilling, exhilarating and fun*. What the wealthy have are opportunities for *purposeful, fulfilling work and positive social roles*.

Much has been written about the diets and lifestyles of cultures characterized by extreme longevity and high levels of health and satisfaction. While many outsiders are obsessed with the diets of Okinawans and Greek islanders, just as important as their diet is their lifestyle, which is rich in *purposeful, fulfilling work and positive social roles*. People in the 80s are still actively tending gardens for hours a day, not because they'll starve if they don't but because they enjoy the work and enjoy sharing the bounty of their labor with their social circle.

Stripping them of the work they enjoy would not just be a cruel punishment; if we understand anything about these cultures, we understand that *enforced leisure* would be a misery-inducing death sentence.

Much has also been written about the unexpected and tragic decline in lifespans of Americans who have lost their jobs to permanent unemployment or under-employment. While commentators collectively wring their hands over the proximate causes—opioid addiction, etc.— what few seem to realize is the devastating consequences of a systemic scarcity of *paid, purposeful work and positive social roles*.

What we need is not Universal Basic Income that gives people just enough to scrape by but no access to capital or opportunity, but a universal *infrastructure of opportunity* that gives everyone opportunities to acquire all the forms of capital needed to have *purposeful work and positive social roles*.

Our goal shouldn't be an impoverished leisure devoid of opportunity; our goal should be to give everyone what the wealthy elites have: not the diamond necklaces, but *agency* (control over one's life), the opportunity to acquire all forms of capital, *fulfilling work and positive social roles*.

Real wealth isn't diamond necklaces; it's having agency and the opportunity to acquire capital, purposeful work and positive social roles. This is what we should guarantee, not the crumbs of UBI.

We can now understand why UBI is morally bankrupt: it's implicitly designed to perpetuate an elitist hierarchy of haves and have-nots. A truly moral system would guarantee access to capital and opportunities for fulfilling work and positive social roles.

UBI's Embrace of Infinite Growth on a Finite Planet

The implicit assumption underpinning Universal Basic Income is that infinite growth on our finite planet is not only possible, but it's necessary to make UBI possible: there must be a ready abundance of consumer essentials for UBI recipients to buy with their monthly cash stipend.

In other words, advocates of UBI (along with conventional economists and pundits) anticipate a science-fiction fairyland of abundant, cheap energy that powers a vast and ever-expanding army of robots that do virtually all the work needed to create surpluses of every material want and need.

Advocates of UBI don't question this science-fiction fairyland of infinite growth on a finite planet; the physics of low-density alternative energy replacing high-density fossil fuels will magically be solved, robots will be as cheap and abundant as energy, and robots will magically perform not just the *profitable work* but all the *unprofitable work* as well.

The reality that robots require immense quantities of costly materials and energy to fabricate, operate and maintain is never mentioned. UBI advocates don't answer this question: who will pay for the robots to perform unprofitable work? Who can afford to fund robots that lose money?

Some readers may feel I'm being overly critical of UBI defenders in targeting their embrace of infinite growth on our finite planet, as they're doing no more than assume the conventional economic model.

But advocates of UBI specifically tout rapid expansion of consumption (as measured by GDP, gross domestic product) as a direct benefit of adopting UBI. For example, the Roosevelt Institute, in conjunction with other economists, published a study in 2017 that claimed UBI of $1,000 a month to every adult would boost U.S. GDP by $2.5 trillion.

An essay by Ellen Brown in *Counterpunch Magazine* exulted in the vast increase in consumption that UBI would generate, as consumers would rapidly increase the velocity of money as they spent their UBI stipend buying up all the goods sitting on the shelves.

By explicitly embracing the model of infinite growth on our finite planet, UBI advocates must answer the same questions directed at all believers of the model: exactly where is all the oil, copper, lithium, tropical hardwood, fertile soil, fresh water, etc. going to come from to fuel this enormous expansion of consumption on a planet whose reserves of fresh water, wild fisheries, oil, etc. are already being depleted?

If we pursue the psychological foundations of these magical infinite-growth assumptions, we find the advocates of UBI are desperate for UBI to be accepted and for it to maintain the status quo that benefits the elite class so handsomely. The fact that UBI presumes that the endless plunder of our planet in service of ever-expanding consumption will never generate any scarcities is too inconvenient to discuss, for it undermines not just the material basis of UBI but its moral claim.

Again, proponents of UBI don't dare question the necessity of plundering the planet or the impossibility of replacing high-density fossil fuels with low-density alternative energy on a planetary scale. The possibility that the planet cannot support infinite growth of consumption would mean facing a future of scarcity and *DeGrowth* rather than endless abundance.

In a world defined by environmental ruin, higher energy costs and scarcity of essentials, the fantasy that a consumerist paradise of cheap abundance awaits every recipient of UBI is as morally bankrupt as the two-tier class hierarchy UBI perpetuates.

The reality of scarcity in an elitist hierarchy is not something the elite class wants to illuminate: the elite class will have full access to what's scarce, and the bottom 90% will have limited or no access to what's scarce.

UBI's Embrace of a Fraudulent Financial System

Just as UBI advocates implicitly assume a science-fiction fairyland of infinite expansion of consumption on a finite planet, they also explicitly embrace the current financial system as the enabler of UBI.

In reality, the current financial system *optimizes income and wealth inequality* and the concentration of wealth and power in the hands of the few (the elite class) at the expense of the many. The core dynamic of our financial system is the creation and distribution of new currency (i.e. money) at the very apex of the wealth-power pyramid: the banking sector, corporations and financiers. Those few with access to cheap, unlimited credit can outbid everyone else for productive assets. Once the ownership of these assets is safely in the hands of the elite class, this class purchases whatever political influence is needed to protect their assets and *rentier* income streams.

This system is credit-based, which simply means that *current consumption is funded by borrowing from future profits and the future extraction of energy*. In effect, our system has substituted debt for actual productive gains for the past 35 years. This is easily visible if we add household and government debt and calculate the debt as a percentage of household median income. The debt per household was 79% of median income in 1980; now it is a staggering 584% of household median income.

In effect, we're piling debt on stagnant household incomes and assets and using the borrowed money to fund our current lifestyle.

The fiction that this system is sustainable is based on the absurd assumption that future profits and energy extraction will grow even faster than our ballooning debt. Put another way: while productivity and real (adjusted for inflation) income are barely edging higher every year, costs are rising by 6% or more annually. We're filling the widening gap between stagnant output/productivity and rising costs with borrowed money.

As I explained in my book *Why the Status Quo Failed and Can't Be Reformed*, this system is not sustainable, nor can it be reformed with the usual policy adjustments. It is corrupt, exploitive, parasitic and profoundly immoral, as its only possible output is *rising income and wealth inequality and debt expanding faster than the ability to service that debt.*

As I have noted many times: *if we don't change the way we create and distribute money, we change nothing.* UBI advocates don't challenge this immoral financial system; rather, they embrace it. As a result, they must answer for the fundamental injustices and immorality of our financial system.

As I will show in the last section of this book, there are alternative models of sustainable growth that are not dependent on debt or central bank issued money distributed to the few at the top.

The Impracticalities of UBI

Now that we've laid bare the conceptual and moral poverty of UBI, let's briefly review the fatal impracticalities of Universal Basic Income.

1. The majority of people don't use their leisure to express themselves artistically or start new enterprises. Entrepreneurism requires an entire ecosystem of support and capital; people can't start enterprises if they lack the capital and the infrastructure.
2. Leisure is not the source of fulfillment or self-realization; *life's work* that provides a positive social role is the source of fulfillment.
3. "Taxing the robots" will not raise the trillions of dollars in new tax revenues that will be needed to fund UBI. Where will the necessary trillions of dollars in new tax revenues come from?
4. Robots cannot replace high-touch work because the value of high-touch work is in the human social contact and communication. Furthermore, great swaths of essential work don't lend themselves to automation.
5. Robots will only perform profitable work, which is a narrow slice of all the work performed in human life. Paying for robots to perform *unprofitable work* makes no financial sense; those who try will be bankrupted.
6. DeGrowth—the contraction of consumption and the revaluation of the intangible capital of community—is the future *Mode of Production*. Localized production and social cohesion is what needs to be fostered and funded, not passive consumption paid by UBI.

Misunderstanding the Economics of Robots

Of the many fatal flaws in the *Universal Basic Income is the solution* world-view, perhaps the most fundamental one is misunderstanding the economics of robots.

In the naïve and superficial view of UBI advocates, substituting robots for human labor not only frees virtually all humans from working, it also generates endless wealth because, well, the robots are doing all the work.

To reach a more realistic understanding of the economics of robots, let's return to author Peter Drucker's maxim: *enterprises don't have profits, enterprises only have expenses*. In other words, from the outside, it looks as if businesses generate profits as a matter of course.

Enterprises don't have profits, enterprises only have expenses captures the core dynamic of all enterprises: the only reliable characteristic of enterprises, whether they are owned by the state, the workers or private investors, is that they have expenses. Profits—needed to reinvest in the enterprise and build capital--can only be reaped if revenues exceed the costs of production, general overhead and debt service.

Robots are complex machines that require substantial quantities of energy and resources to produce, program and maintain. As a result, they will never be super-cheap to manufacture, own or maintain.

Robots, and the ecosystem of software, engineering, spare parts, diagnostics, etc. needed to produce, power and maintain them, are a large capital and operational expense.

The greater the complexity of the tasks the robot is designed to complete, the greater the complexity and cost of the robot.

Robots only make financial sense in a very narrow swath of commoditized production, or in situations such as war or hazardous rescue missions where cost is not the primary issue.

Compare the following two tasks and the cost and complexity of the robots needed to complete them in a cost-effective manner.

Task one: move boxes around a warehouse with flat concrete floors and fixed shelving mounted with hundreds of sensors to guide robots.

Task two: navigate extremely rough and uneven terrain with no embedded sensors, dig deep holes in rocky soil, and plant a delicate seedling in each hole. Each hole must be selected by contextual criteria; there is no pre-set grid pattern to the planting.

The first task has all the features that make robots cost-effective: easily navigable flat floors, fixed, easily mapped structures embedded with multiple sensors, and a limited, easily programmable repertoire of physical movements: stock boxes on the shelving, retrieve boxes from the shelving. The compact working space makes it practical to reprogram, recharge and repair the robots; spare parts can be kept onsite, and so on.

The second task—one of the steps in restoring a habitat—has none of these features. The terrain is extremely uneven and challenging to navigate; the varied surfaces may be hazardous in non-obvious ways (prone to sliding, etc.); there are no embedded sensors to guide the robot; it's difficult and costly to service the robots onsite, and the task is extremely contextual, requiring numerous judgments and decisions and a wide variety of physical steps, ranging from the arduous task of digging a hole in rocky ground to delicately handling fragile seedlings.

Exactly what sort of robot would be capable of completing these tasks without human guidance? A drone might be able to ferry the fragile seedlings, but any drone capable of landing and punching a hole in unforgiving ground would be very heavy. Combining these disparate skills in one or even multiple robots—the heavy work of digging a hole in rocky soil on uneven ground, embedding a fragile seedling in just the right amount of compost and then watering the seedling deeply enough to give it a chance to survive—would be technically challenging.

And what profit is there to be earned from this restoration a public-land habitat? Since the habitat is public commons, there is no customer base to sell high-margin products to. If the state is paying for the job, it chooses the vendor by competitive bidding. Given the conditions, a vendor with human labor will likely be more reliable and cheaper, as this is the sort of work that humans are supremely adapted to perform efficiently. Given that restoring a habitat generates no profit, perhaps the work is done entirely by volunteers.

In any of these cases, a costly array of robots facing a daunting challenge that could cause multiple failures (robots sliding down the slope, seedlings crushed, too little compost, compost over-compressed, water didn't soak in, etc.) is simply not cost-effective.

You see the point: humans have few advantages in a concrete floored warehouse with fixed metal shelving. Robots have all the advantages in that carefully controlled environment performing repeatable, easily defined tasks. But in the wilds of a hillside jumble of rocks, fallen trees, etc., handling tasks that require accuracy, strength, judgment, contextual understanding and a delicate touch, humans have all the advantages.

In other words, robots are only cost-effective in the narrow niches of *commoditized tasks*: repeatable tasks that are easy to break down into programmable steps that can be performed in a controlled environment.

Those with little experience of actually manufacturing a robot may look at a multi-million dollar prototype performing some task (often under human guidance, which is carefully kept off-camera) and assume that robots will decline in price on the same trajectory as computer components.

But the geometric rise in computing power and the corresponding decline in the cost of processing and memory is not a model for real-world components such as robots, which will continue to be extraordinarily resource and energy-intensive even if microchips decline in cost.

Vehicles might be a more realistic example of the cost consequences of increasing complexity and the consumption of resources: vehicles haven't declined in cost by 95% like memory chips; they've increased in cost.

Self-driving vehicles are another example of how commoditized automation can be profitable performing a commoditized task. First, roadways are smooth, easy to map and easy to embed with sensors. Second, vehicles are intrinsically complex and costly; the average price of a vehicle is around $40,000. The sensors, electronics, software and motors required to make a vehicle autonomous are a relatively modest percentage of the total cost of the vehicle. Third, manufacturing vehicles is a profitable venture with a large base of customers. Fourth, the actual tasks of driving—navigating streets, accelerating, braking, etc.—are relatively limited in number. In other words, driving is a *commoditized task* that lends itself to automation.

Once again, robots have multiple advantages in this *commoditized task* as they are not easily distracted, don't get drunk, and they don't fall asleep. Humans have few advantages in this environment. And as noted, manufacturing autonomous vehicles will likely be a highly profitable business for those who master the processes.

Since so much of the production of goods and services in the advanced economies is based on *commoditized tasks*, it's easy to make the mistake of extending these very narrowly defined capabilities in profitable enterprises to the whole of human life. But as my example illustrates, a wide array of work doesn't lend itself to *cost-effective* robots, as robots have few if any advantages in these environments, while humans are supremely adapted to doing these kinds of tasks.

But this is not the truly crushing limitation of robots; that limit is economic.

Marx described the consequences of over-investment in *commoditized production* and the resulting over-capacity: when anyone with access to investors or credit can buy the same machinery—that is, the machines are interchangeable commodities such as sewing machines, power looms, etc.--the capacity to produce rises as every competitor attempts to lower the unit cost of each product by producing more.

In other words, the only competitive advantage in an economy of commoditized machines and products is to increase production by over-investing in productive capacity. If competition has lowered the price of products, those who can double their production will achieve profitable economies of scale.

Over-investment and overcapacity are intrinsic dynamics of production; those who fail to invest heavily in increasing capacity will become unprofitable. Once their capital is destroyed, they vanish in insolvency.

As Marx explained, every enterprise is driven to pursue the same strategy, and the end result is massive over-investment and overcapacity. The flood of products overwhelms demand, and prices fall below the production costs.

Over-investment leads to overcapacity that devalues whatever is being produced.

This leads to a counter-intuitive result: *over-investment destroys capital.*

The naïve faith that robots will generate so much wealth that humans will have no work has it backward: *over-investment in commoditized robots and their commoditized production will destroy capital, not create it.*

Recall that *enterprises don't have profits, enterprises only have expenses.* Robots will never be free, due to their intrinsic complexity and use of resources and energy. As robots and other tools of automation become commodities that anyone can buy, whatever robots can produce is devalued accordingly. In other words, *whatever commoditized robots can produce is no longer profitable; rather, the production destroys capital.*

This leads to a startling conclusion: *this destruction of capital must be subsidized by taxing whatever is still profitable,* i.e. *whatever cannot be commoditized or automated.*

In other words, enterprises profiting from human labor that can't be replaced by commoditized (interchangeable) robots will be subsidizing intrinsically unprofitable robotic production that destroys capital.

Exactly how will all these robots create unimaginable wealth when every moment they're in production they're destroying capital? It will fall to the remaining profitable enterprises and their human employees to subsidize the capital-destroying robots.

Robots can only perform profitable work, and in a fully commoditized production chain, very little production will be profitable. This raises a question: who will subsidize all the unprofitable robots? Who will buy them, program them, repair them and energize them? Who will subsidize all this capital-destroying work performed by robots?

Robots Will Only Perform Work That Is Profitable

Those who foresee robots doing virtually all work currently performed by humans overlook a fundamental limiting factor: robots will only perform work that is profitable. As noted above, robots are intrinsically costly to manufacture, program, power and maintain. No enterprise can afford to manufacture, buy and operate robots that lose money.

The basic premise of profitable robots is that the profit is reaped by replacing costly human labor. In the initial stages, this is true: a robot that replaces a human worker, and the robot costs less than the annual wage and overhead of a human factory worker, the replacement will be profitable to the owner of the robot.

But as explained above, once robots become interchangeable commodities, i.e. something anyone can buy and program, competitors will invest in increasing their productive capacity with robots, and the resulting competition will reduce prices. As over-investment and overcapacity reduce the value of whatever is being produced, profits turn to losses and capital is destroyed by overcapacity.

So the initial profits reaped by replacing humans are quickly eroded as competitors automate their own production.

As noted earlier, only a limited spectrum of human labor is paid. Unprofitable work is not paid for the same reason robots will not be purchased to do unprofitable work: whomever pays people or robots to perform unprofitable work will go broke.

This means that a wide spectrum of human labor can't be replaced by robots because the work is not even paid, so there's no profit to be reaped by replacing the human labor.

Also as noted earlier, *the value of high-touch work is that it is performed by a human.* People pay for high-touch work precisely because the value is in the human contact and communication. The entire value proposition is the human presence, so replacing a human with a robot destroys the value and thus the profitability. As explained above, people will accept low-touch tasks being automated because the value proposition is not in the human contact. But they're willing to pay the higher costs of high-touch services precisely to avoid robots and automated systems.

In a consumer society that's centered on convenience and signifiers of status, it's widely assumed that consumers with surplus income will buy robots to replace human service workers. The manufacture and distribution of millions of household robots is presumed to be enviably profitable.

But there are limits on this supposed profitability. One limitation is the number of households with enough surplus income to buy a multi-functional, programmable robot, i.e. a robot that can do more than scoot around the room vacuuming up everything in its path. Only the top 5% of households (roughly 6 million) have enough income and wealth to buy a costly status-symbol robot to perform low-value conventional household duties.

A rather limited programmable factory-floor robot currently costs around $35,000. A mobile robot costs more. Even with the expected reductions in price as volume increases, it will never be low-cost to construct and maintain a robot that can navigate uneven terrain, for example, and do all the tasks a human gardener performs—trimming the hedge, weeding the garden, dead-heading the roses, and so on. The complexity of a robot capable of performing all these tasks on uneven terrain is intrinsically high, and so the cost can't be reduced much by economies of scale.

The point is that repeatable, low-touch work lends itself to commoditization via robots/automation, but not all work can be commoditized. Robots are optimized for specific types of work, while humans are exquisitely adapted to do the kinds of work that can't be commoditized.

Simply put, robots can't do every task currently performed by humans in a cost-effective fashion.

In other words, their intrinsic cost and complexity limits the profitability of robots. Replacing a $50,000 a year human factory worker with a $35,000 robot makes compelling sense to an enterprise facing competitors who are automating their production, but buying (and maintaining) a $35,000 robot to do household work that's only worth a few hundred dollars when performed by a human makes no financial sense.

Needless to say, low-income households will not have the means to buy robots, so the idea that robots marketed as status symbols for the wealthy will transform the economy is false.

In summary: robots will only do work that is profitable, and as robots become commoditized, the value of their output will plummet, along with the profits generated by that output. As explained above, overcapacity destroys capital and profits. Robots only make financial sense in very narrow fields of commoditized production. Unpaid work will not be replaced by robots, nor will work that cannot be commoditized for which humans are optimized.

But robots and automation have another whole set of limitations. As noted in the section on *What Do the Wealthy Have that the Poor Don't Have?*, value flows to what's scarce, and commoditized products and services generated by commoditized robots have near-zero scarcity value. So what's scarce and valuable isn't automation; what's scarce and valuable are solutions to the problems of over-consumption, exploitation of the Earth's resources by profit-maximizing economies and the degradation of human communities.

The overcapacity intrinsic to automation destroys financial capital, globalized commoditization destroys social capital, and overconsumption destroys the planet's natural capital. The fantasy that robots will do all the work of stripmining the Earth to provide for our endless overconsumption, and generate vast profits doing so, is just another manifestation of an intrinsically destructive and unsustainable *Mode of Production.*

Where Will the Trillions for UBI Come From?

Advocates of UBI are long on idealistic abstractions and short on real-world line-item specifics when it comes to where the immense sums needed to fund Universal Basic Income will come from.

Let's assemble the most basic economic and demographic facts about the U.S. and the most straightforward proposals for UBI and work from there.

While some advocate replacing all social entitlements such as Social Security with UBI, this doesn't generate new revenue, In other words, the Social Security system distributes about $1 trillion in benefits annually to roughly 70 million retirees. If this program were replaced by UBI, the cost would remain around the same sum (or perhaps it might be higher, if the UBI monthly payment exceeded the median Social Security monthly payment).

For simplicity's sake, let's set the existing retirement and healthcare programs for those 65 and older aside—Social Security and Medicare— as well as healthcare programs such as Medicaid and the Veterans Administration healthcare system, since most UBI proposals do not include healthcare. Let's also leave the existing programs in support of children aside, and define UBI as a simple monthly cash disbursement to all adults 16 to 64. In the U.S. this is around 200 million individuals.

How much money does an individual need in the U.S. to secure shelter, food, utilities, some form of transport, etc.? The problem is that the costs of these basics vary widely depending on the region: an individual in New York City or San Francisco will need double or even triple the sum that is sufficient for a rural resident in a low-cost state.

Assuming the UBI payment is based on some metric of local costs, we'll choose an average monthly sum, averaging out the most costly and most affordable regions. For simplicity's sake, let's start with $1,000 a month per individual. That's $12,000 per year for 200 million individuals, or $2.4 trillion.

One commonly accepted tenet of UBI is that existing social welfare programs will be replaced with UBI. In the U.S., this could include unemployment insurance, food stamps (SNAP), and housing subsidies. These programs cost around $200 billion, so the net cost for UBI would be around $2.2 trillion.

Assuming the UBI is taxed as conventional income, those individuals with other sources of income will pay a percentage of their UBI in taxes. For example, if an individual earning $50,000 receives $12,000 in UBI, he will pay taxes on $62,000 in total income.

The effective federal tax rate—the rate paid after deductions and credits—varies by income bracket, from 3.9% for the bottom 20% of taxpayers to 25% for the top 5% and 31% for the top 1% (according to date from the Peter G. Peterson Foundation). The average is roughly 18%. So as a rough estimate, we can anticipate about 20% of all UBI payments will be returned to the Treasury as conventional tax revenues.

This comes to about $440 billion annually. Thus the net cost of UBI for all adults drops from $2.2 trillion to around $1.75 trillion.

The current (2017) federal budget is about $4.1 trillion, and federal tax receipts are around $3.6 trillion, mostly paid by payroll taxes on wage earners (85%); corporate taxes are 10% ($355 billion) and other taxes make up the remaining 5%. The $500 billion deficit is borrowed from future taxpayers via the sale of Treasury bonds (future taxpayers must pay interest on the debt we leave them).

State and local government expenditures total an additional $3.2 trillion. Total government expenditures are thus about $7.3 trillion annually, around 39% of the nation's Gross Domestic Product (GDP) of $18.5 trillion.

(Some state and local government social welfare programs might also be replaced by UBI, but since much of the local government social welfare funding is provided by federal agencies, this becomes a very complex calculation that is beyond the scope of this basic accounting.)

Returning to federal taxes: adding $1.75 trillion in net UBI costs means federal tax receipts will have to rise by 50%, from $3.6 trillion to $5.35 trillion. The additional $1.75 trillion pushes the total government share of GDP to 49%: of the $18.5 trillion GDP, $9.05 trillion will be government expenditures.

Denmark currently has one of the highest government-to-GDP ratio, around 50%. (Note that Denmark isn't funding a Universal Basic Income.) UBI would push the U.S. into this same range.

The question then becomes: who will pay the additional $1.75 trillion in taxes needed to fund UBI? Taxation is a zero-sum game: the taxes the government collects come out of someone's pocket, and is then distributed to others' pockets. To fund UBI, some portion of the taxpaying populace will have considerably less to spend, save or invest.

This is where unintended consequences come into play. Many advocate raising corporate taxes to pay for UBI. Let's suppose corporate taxes doubled. Not only does that only raise $355 billion of the needed $1.75 trillion, that means returns on private pension funds will decline sharply, punishing funds that depend on high returns in U.S. stocks. Doubling corporate taxes will only add to the existing incentives to relocate or leave profits overseas.

What happens to investment in productivity gains when a significant portion of the nation's GDP is shifted to individuals via UBI? There are many complexities to consider, and the primary point here is the economy is dynamic and interconnected, and it's very difficult to predict what unintended consequences might arise.

Consider the oft-repeated (but never substantiated) claim that *taxing the robots* will fund UBI. To the degree that automation is already an integral component of productivity, we're already taxing the robots/software. A heavy tax levied on production robots will create an unavoidable incentive to move production robots overseas to evade the U.S. tax.

As other commentators have pointed out, the entire concept of taxing the robots is riddled with inconsistencies and unintended consequences. Since automation (robotics, software, artificial intelligence, etc.) is the key to increasing productivity and thus prosperity in knowledge-based economies, taxing these tools to raise $1.75 trillion annually would punish the very engines of productivity needed to fund such an enormous increase in taxes.

It's also impossible to clearly delineate between the tools of automation that augment human labor (creating more job opportunities and productivity) and those that replace human labor.

All of this assumes payrolls and corporate taxes will remain at their current lofty levels. But there are two automation-generated dynamics at work that will reduce tax revenues, possibly drastically. The first is that *commoditization reduces profits*. As the tools of automation become commoditized—mass produced, available everywhere, interchangeable—the scarcity value of these tools declines to zero, along with profit margins.

Once anyone can buy the same robots and software tools, then competition inevitably drives profit margins to near-zero, as there is no pricing power in owning commoditized tools.

Secondly, as software chews it way up the labor ladder, automating higher skills, payrolls stagnate or decline, reducing the primary source of taxes. This is already evident in the secular stagnation in the number of full-time private-sector jobs, which only recently edged above the level of 2008, ten years ago.

As I have explained many times in the blog and in my books, the majority of the growth of the global economy in the 21st century has been fueled by unprecedented expansions of debt and leverage. The proponents of UBI assume that debt can continue to grow to the sky and then to the moon. Less intoxicated observers have concluded that borrowing $100 to eke out a $1 gain in GDP is not a sustainable dynamic, as the vast speculative bubbles and mal-investments that are the fruits of this global debt expansion are inherently unstable.

One of the two dynamics of debt expansion will lead to a global recession in which sales, profits and tax revenues plummet and defaults soar: either debt expansion slows, or the returns on further debt expansion diminish to the point that additional debt and speculation actually cripples productivity.

In other words, just maintaining tax revenues at their current levels will be increasingly challenging, never mind increase them by $1.75 trillion annually.

As I have often noted in my previous books, the appealing idea of taxing the wealthy to raise the $1.75 trillion in revenue needed to fund UBI ignores the political reality that the super-wealthy and corporations have purchased political power with campaign contributions, lobbying, revolving door cronyism between government and private industry, and the funding of influential think tanks and foundations, i.e. *philanthro-capitalism*.

The super-wealthy have the financial and political means to evade such taxes. This is the consequence of our pay-to-play form of representative democracy: wealth casts the votes that count. It would be a major political victory to raise even $100 billion more in tax revenues from the super-wealthy. Given this reality, the idea of skimming $1.75 trillion annually from the super-wealthy isn't even remotely realistic.

According to Internal Revenue Service (IRS) data, the top 1% received about 20% of the nation's $10 trillion in income: $2 trillion. To raise the entire $1.75 trillion cost of UBI, the vast majority of the super-wealthy's income would have to be skimmed as tax revenues. As noted above, this isn't politically realistic.

Since much of the financial elites' wealth and income flows from asset bubbles, when these bubbles burst (as they inevitably do, due to the intrinsic limits on the efficacy of ballooning debt), then the wealth and income of the elite will plummet sharply, reducing their total income below the needed $1.75 trillion.

In conclusion, there is no practical way to raise the additional $1.75 trillion annually needed to fund UBI without triggering a host of unintended consequences that could undermine the very engines of profit and productivity that taxation depends on.

UBI's Consequences: Dependence, Social Depression, Inflation and Debt-Serfdom

Very few (if any) advocates of Universal Basic Income have addressed the potentially adverse consequences of no-strings attached monthly cash payments. Advocates naturally prefer to claim that UBI will make everyone happy because they will no longer have to worry about earning a livelihood.

One is the impact on the motivation of recipients to pursue productive pathways such as starting new enterprises, a topic discussed below. While advocates of UBI are keen to stress the freeing-from-want benefit of UBI, they are less keen to explore the possibility that UBI weakens the motivation to be productive in ways that benefit the recipient and the community.

There is a decided dearth of evidence that UBI by itself leads to higher rates of entrepreneurship, volunteerism in the community, or other metrics of productive engagement. In other words, there is little evidence that UBI increases the *social capital* of the community. Rather,

UBI nurtures a culture and mindset of consumerist dependence and erodes self-reliance as recipients naturally turn to the state to provide for them.

As I have explained, UBI has no mechanism for creating an *infrastructure of opportunity* (i.e. pathways to capital accumulation) for individuals, or for building social capital within a community. UBI's only mechanism is to fund consumption.

UBI's implicit assumption is that the market will provide for all needs via consumer choice, and so the only necessary ingredient for social cohesion is a cash stipend distributed to individuals.

The second implicit assumption of UBI is that whatever the market doesn't provide via "the invisible hand" of consumer choice will be magically provided by centralized government.

Both of these assumptions are tragically false.

As I have endeavored to explain, giving cash stipends to individuals is a boon to corporations that need customers for their goods and services, but this atomized consumption generates *social depression* and *social defeat*, not happiness and fulfillment.

Humans need to be needed, and they need positive social roles that lead to the betterment of their lives and families. Merely distributing cash stipends provides nothing we need beyond material survival, and neither the market nor the state transforms atomized consumers into cohesive communities.

Consider the trajectory of contemporary consumption-based capitalism. In a community economy, Main Street was composed of numerous independent shop owners and producers. These enterprises were local, meaning that the owners of capital lived and worked in the community itself. The surpluses from this capital (i.e. profit) stayed in the community. The children of small business owners went to school with the customers' children, and the owners of local capital (shops, farms, bakeries, accounting offices, etc.) had a built-in incentive to support their community by funding the Boy Scouts, Girl Scouts, holiday parades to the town square, and so on—the many-layered web of social contacts, obligations and sharing that together form a cohesive community.

This localized economy had the proximity, understanding of local conditions and capital to address local scarcities in ways that fit the culture and economy.

Then globalized capital and supply chains arrived in the form of Walmart, a centralized corporate quasi-monopoly that destroyed Main Street and siphoned all the community's profit and overhead to corporate headquarters and shareholders. Needless to say, the corporate managers and hedge fund managers who benefited immensely from this siphoning of local capital did not live in the towns they eviscerated.

Walmart and other corporate quasi-monopolies had no incentive to fund local community groups, and no mechanism to recognize, much less address, local scarcities in social capital. Global corporations donate a thin slice of their profits for PR purposes to centralized philanthro-capitalist foundations and do-gooder approved environmental non-profits.

Capital is drained from the local economy, which becomes impoverished, not just in financial capital, but in social capital and intellectual capital—the knowledge and skills needed to start and operate enterprises, organize local efforts to benefit the community and meet local scarcities.

The centralized government also has no incentive or mechanisms to recognize or address the draining of local capital or the resulting scarcities of social capital. The government tracks the decline in tax revenues as local capital bleeds away, and welcomes the corporate quasi-monopoly as a tax base.

But as Marx so succinctly noted, capitalism turns everything that is solid into air, and even the solidity of Walmart dissipates into thin air once stores don't measure up to the corporate demands for *high profits, always*.

Now the Amazon model of vast distribution centers staffed by robots and low-paid workers and a distribution network that is slated to feature delivery-via-drone is driving the Walmart model to extinction in local economies.

To the proponents of Universal Basic Income, this eradication of the local economy in favor of centralized global capital doesn't even register, as their entire focus is on consumption rather than on social capital and production. In their myopic view, if UBI enables individuals to pay for goods shipped to their door by Amazon drones, then UBI has provided everything necessary for human fulfillment and happiness: the material basics and leisure time.

As I have explained at length, atomized consumption of corporate globalized goods does not magically generate positive social roles for recipients of UBI. UBI lacks any mechanism to recognize the critical roles of social capital and positive social roles, other than an idealized belief that these forms of capital will magically spring to life out of leisure.

As noted previously, this is like dropping someone into a parched desert with $1,000 and expecting them to create a lush, productive farm because they now have leisure time to fill. Once the complex web of capital required to nurture enterprises and social cohesion is lost, expecting individuals given a cash stipend and free time to create all this capital on their own is a flight of absurd fantasy.

If any advocate of UBI thinks this is possible, I invite them to move to a region stripped of all forms of capital, a community with little collective memory of self-reliance, a region reduced to atomized individuals receiving UBI that they use to buy essentials, and recreate all that was lost when Main Street, vibrant public spaces and positive social roles were destroyed, all on their monthly UBI stipend of $1,000.

Given the perverse incentives generated by UBI and the impoverishment of the region by global capital, the UBI advocate who imagines leisure time is all that's needed to rebuild social capital and positive social roles will learn the hard way that the global-capital Mode of Production system he/she embraces has created a desert of social depression and defeat.

Many advocates of UBI falsely assume that UBI will recreate the social-welfare zeitgeist of small Scandinavian states such as Denmark and Sweden. Overlooking the source of these states' wealth—capital accumulated via colonial-era exploitation, globalized trade and unsustainable dependence on debt-fueled speculative bubbles in housing and other assets—a more fine-grained understanding of the social aspects of these welfare systems reveals a strong social-capital framework. Sweden, for example, encourages people to re-enter the workforce, and the system makes an extraordinary effort to create new jobs and industries for displaced workers.

In other words, the success of these social-welfare systems is not the result of the mere distribution of cash stipends, i.e. Universal Basic Income, but of a complex social structure that includes incentives and obligations that extend beyond mere consumption.

As I explain in my book *Resistance, Revolution, Liberation*, UBI also breeds a culture of complicity with the state; recipients of UBI are much less likely to be politically independent if they fear their UBI stipend might be at risk. Stripped of niceties, UBI is a mechanism of co-option and complicity, a centralized means of control based on buying the compliance of the citizenry.

Proponents are also blind to the likelihood that UBI will trigger inflation in the very basics the program is supposed to secure, defeating the intended purpose.

Current needs-based housing subsidies provide an example of this dynamic. Once the federal government's subsidized housing program sets the minimum rent that will be paid for qualified recipients, private-sector rent rise to that new minimum. The reason is self-evident: why should property managers accept less than the federally mandated minimum, when they can guarantee that rent by entering the program?

It's not difficult to foresee the same dynamic occurring once UBI sets a minimum income that enables increased competition for desirable housing: a modest apartment that fetched $400 will quickly rise to $500 as UBI recipients with other sources of income outbid UBI-only recipients, and some UBI beneficiaries opt to sacrifice other spending to afford better living quarters.

In other words, the net effect of UBI is to flood local economies with additional cash without increasing the local production of goods and services. This is the classic engine of inflation: an increase in the amount of money chasing a quantity of goods and services that hasn't increased.

Advocates of UBI are equally blind to the possibility that the secure income stream provided by UBI will be siphoned off by exploitive lending practices designed to appeal to recipients' natural desire to buy now and pay later. Once again, this dynamic is already visible in high-interest-rate credit cards and similar predatory lending practices.

The ability to forsake instant gratification in service of long-term goals is not innate; it must be learned. UBI's monthly stipend will not magically impart the discipline needed to override short-term gratification to meet long-term goals via sacrifice and planning.

The net effect of this dynamic is to transform UBI recipients into *debt-serfs*, as a substantial portion of their monthly cash income will be devoted to debt service rather than the intended basics.

Though it is politically hazardous to even raise the topic, the possibility that a significant percentage of UBI recipients might not choose to allocate their new cash income responsibly cannot be ignored in light of the lessons learned from existing social welfare programs, which have evolved to limit recipients' leeway to spend the benefit on non-essentials.

This is not to pass any sort of moral judgment on the very common human practice of spending available cash to gratify short-term desires, it is simply to note that existing social welfare programs such as SNAP (food stamps) and housing vouchers intentionally limit the recipients' freedom to spend the benefit on anything but the intended purpose—food and housing.

If we combine these readily-foreseeable dynamics, we reach another troubling prospect: the isolation of UBI recipients who have no other source of income in areas avoided by recipients of UBI who have additional sources of earned income.

Such isolation adds to the potential for *behavioral sinks*, a term for the collapse of community that results from there being fewer positive social roles than residents, a structure I term *social depression* and *social defeat*.

All of these unintended consequences of UBI are studiously avoided by advocates, a selective blindness that undermines the well-intentioned but unsubstantiated claims of UBI proponents that distributing cash stipends will magically create universal fulfillment and happiness.

Emotional Appeal Is Not a Substitute for Practical Policy

I understand the emotional appeal of Universal Basic Income: UBI appears to be a simple, moral solution to the insecurities generated by an automated Mode of Production. But emotional appeal is not a substitute for analysis. Stripped of sentimentality, emotional appeal is just another marketing strategy of consumerism: this is how we sell things, by generating superficial emotional appeal.

In effect, UBI is the policy equivalent of photos of puppies and kittens: isn't it adorable, the nice robots will make everything for us, we'll tax the nice robots and live happily ever after in everlasting abundance.

I share the goal of providing universal security, and find photos of puppies and kittens as adorable as the next person, and I understand the need to market a new policy in an emotionally appealing manner. But any policy that claims to be a solution for complex, systemic problems must first prove its readiness for the real world.

Emotional attachment to the goal of UBI doesn't magically render UBI workable. Rather, the emotional loyalty generated by the worthy ideal blinds us to the uncomfortable realities that UBI is the opposite of what its idealistic supporters envision: it institutionalizes an unsustainable two-tier society of an elite class with access to all that's scarce and a permanent underclass stripped of capital and opportunity, scraping by on UBI.

We now turn a critical light on the specific claims that generate much of UBI's emotional appeal: that creative self-expression will replace work; that creative self-expression can generate extra income for millions of people, and that UBI will subsidize entrepreneurship.

The Fantasy of Creative Self-Expression Replacing Work

I was watching a video discussion of the merits of Universal Basic Income, and one of the panel members—a tenured professor with an ample income, the respect of his peers and a high-status social role, i.e. a typical advocate of UBI—opined that the recipients of UBI (and I paraphrase here) would write poetry, most of it bad (a note of elitist condescension), but some of it would be good, and everyone would be happy.

This perfectly encapsulates the conventional view of UBI proponents: everyone will write poetry (or an artistic equivalent), most of the poetry will be bad but a few good poems will emerge. This process of writing poetry/artistic expression will be deeply satisfying for the tens of millions of individuals freed by UBI.

Question One: do you know even one person who fills even one day composing poetry? How about a week? A month? A year? Have you ever tried to fill even one day writing poetry?

The belief that creative expression is a satisfying substitute for productive work is utterly groundless, and ignores everything we know about human nature and happiness. Only a handful of extremely driven people spend their days composing poetry or equivalent artistic endeavors. These few do so regardless of their income or need to earn a livelihood.

Recall our example of the laid-off housepainter who enjoyed painting landscapes. After a few hours alone in front of his canvas, he hungered for the old satisfactions of working productively with his comrades. He found satisfaction not in dabbling with art but in contributing to the after-school art program, which gave him everything that isolated artistic expression did not: a positive social role, human engagement, high-touch work.

On a personal note: I have decades of experience with both of the presumed activities of those freed from earning a livelihood by UBI: creative expression and entrepreneurship. I know firsthand how difficult it is to face a blank page/canvas/recorder and create some new content/art/music, day after day, week after week, month after month, and year after year. I know how few people who attempt this lifestyle sustain it despite a lack of commercial recognition and success. I know firsthand how difficult it is to earn any money from creating content/art.

I also know the extreme challenges of starting a new small business and nurturing it to self-sustaining success, i.e. it generates enough revenues to pay all the bills, all the employees and all the taxes, and leaves enough left over for my own paycheck (or not, in many cases).

I notice that few if any of the proponents of UBI who expect recipients will become artists and/or entrepreneurs are themselves self-supporting artists or entrepreneurs. From the idealized heights of those with no direct experience of *creating content/art as one's life's work* or of starting a small business without the support of a network of mentors, family and investors, it certainly looks romantically appealing.

Few if any of the proponents of the claim that *UBI will free everyone to become artists or entrepreneurs* appear to have looked into what it takes to actually fulfill their romantic fantasies, or done any research on how many people from unprivileged backgrounds forge fulfilling lives in the arts or as entrepreneurs. Few if any UBI advocates seem to realize the key factor is not the material security promised by UBI but access to the wealth of capital I described as the *infrastructure of opportunity*.

The Democratization of Artistic Expression

A brief review of artistic expression in the modern era will shed some light on the baseless assumption that the only thing holding people back from becoming an artist is a lack of guaranteed basic income.

In the pre-modern economy (that is to say, pre-Industrial Revolution, pre-financialization), artists, composers and writers were typically supported by wealthy patrons—aristocrats or the church. Some of these creators labored as private tutors, university readers, concert masters or church music directors; others were commissioned to complete specific works of art.

As the Renaissance broadened the middle class, a few creators were able to support themselves via marketing their art to wealthy individuals. Some (for example, Rembrandt) established workshops that produced quantities of art that was sold under the master's imprint.

The Industrial Revolution saw another rapid expansion of the middle class, and the broadening of access to the arts via the commoditization of art (lithograph prints), literature and poetry (inexpensive books) and eventually, music via phonographs and radio.

The rise of an educated, prosperous bourgeois class between the owners of capital and the working class enabled a flowering of artistic aspirations, because more families could afford to support the arts and their children's artistic endeavors.

The educated person of 1900 had more information and energy (artificial lighting, transport, etc.) at his/her fingertips than nobility possessed in the pre-modern era. The resulting freedom of expression powered Modernism: rather than blindly accepting the interpretations of authorities, one should seek one's own interpretations.

However, such dissolution of certainties is obviously dangerous, for the reason noted by the novelist Fyodor Dostoevsky: *If there is no God, everything is permitted.* Friedrich Nietzsche also had a knack for catchy phrases that captured key elements of "Question Everything" Modernism: *God is dead* and *Man/Superman* (*ubermensch*).

This focus on the individual discovery of Truth defined Nietzsche's entire project. With certainty dead, it was now up to each individual to pursue his/her own interpretation of Truth.

It was no great leap from this to the idea of a Superman, an individual who was beyond the reach of conventions, a person who made their own truths and rules.

This idea of a Superman arising from internal characteristics rather than recognized authority is an extraordinarily modern idea. Prior to this, certain individuals were imbued with what we might call the superpowers of divine or semi-divine authority, but these powers were bestowed by institutions: the church or the state, which can be viewed as a secular church in which emperors, kings and queens assumed divine authority.

This leveling of authority extended to the judgment of what qualified as worthy art, music, poetry and literature. The artistic authority that defined talent and value was cast aside in favor of tradition-breaking modernist art (for example, cubism), which captured the imagination of bourgeois taste-makers, who also declared difficult novels (for example, *Ulysses* by James Joyce) modern masterpieces. Dissonant, unmelodic music broke down the citadel of classical music, and jazz became the favored form of popular music.

The natural extension of this Modernism was the idea that *all creative efforts are essentially equal,* provided the creator was earnestly seeking his/her own truth. Any effort to differentiate the output as somehow superior (i.e. more revolutionary, more Modern) was suspect, as Modernist judgments were as open to question as any pre-Modern certainties.

The dissolution of critical authority led to two developments:

1. The ascendancy of the marketplace in deciding what was revolutionary and (most importantly) desirable, and
2. The ascendancy of Post-Modernism, which sought a contingent and ambiguous meaning in the subtexts not just of artistic output, but also in the criticism of art.

In this post-modern world, anyone could be an artist, writer, poet, filmmaker, composer, choreographer, dancer, actor/actress, playwright, designer, photographer, etc. Those who didn't create could become critics of the creators. No one was excluded, and this democratizing of creative endeavors and criticism promised an unprecedented outpouring of art and criticism.

Now the World Wide Web has extended this democratization, making it essentially free to post both creative output and criticism, and this has fueled the bourgeois notion that everyone freed from the burdens of earning a living will naturally become creators or critics in their now-abundant spare time.

Why is this a fantasy?

Let's start with a question: how many people do you know who spend 40 hours a week, month after month, year after year, writing novels nobody wants to read, painting canvases nobody wants to buy, composing music nobody wants to listen to, making films nobody wants to watch or writing criticism nobody cares to read?

I think we all know the answer is effectively zero. Those few who are so driven to create their art that an absence of positive feedback from peers and customers does not deter them are very few in number.

It turns out that artistic self-expression does not boil down to the democratization of leisure. There are extraordinary differences in talent, drive and creativity between people who enjoy equal access to knowledge and the marketplace.

The idea that creative self-expression will be a substitute for fulfilling work is absurd on multiple levels. Not only are few people equipped to create full-time, even fewer have the capacity to sustain their output in a vacuum of positive feedback.

The fantasy is promulgated by the intellectual class who dreams of all the wonderful art, novels, music, etc. they would create if only they were free of the burdens of a demanding job.

As appealing as this idea is to well-paid intellectuals, the reality is sobering: those few that are equipped to create art on a full-time basis do so whether they have a job or not.

The idea that creative self-expression is a ready substitute for work is also a fantasy because creating art that isn't appreciated doesn't generate a positive social role, the respect of peers, or an identity grounded in one's contribution to others.

There is one group of people who have an income that isn't derived from work we can use as an example: trust fund recipients. Trust funders are a class of people who are freed from the toil of paid work because they draw monthly income from a family trust. By studying this fortunate group, we can field-test the notion that having the leisure to create will make people much happier and more creative than having to work.

Trust funders are, in effect, recipients of guaranteed basic income. We might expect to find them by and large much happier than the working populace, and much more devoted to artistic self-expression.

Though I can't locate any reliable statistics on this, anecdotally, trust funders seem to be dabblers and dilettantes who flit from one project to the next, never finishing the novels, canvases and compositions they start. Many, if not most, are plagued by one form of chronic unhappiness or another, as their abundance of free time is largely devoted to narcissism, medications and angst.

The other pool of people who have no work due to a guaranteed income and abundant free time are welfare recipients. Granted, the income is modest, but a self-directed artist would work with whatever tools and materials were available—and in today's world, tools and materials can often be scavenged for free, borrowed, or bought used for pennies on the dollar.

Yet if we review the output of welfare recipients, we find an absence of art—and an abundance of social dysfunctions. It is easy to say these result from the poverty of the recipients' upbringing and circumstances, but this is more of an excuse than an explanation: the classic artist in the cold-water unheated attic is a whirlwind of creativity, despite his/her poverty.

The reality is the vast majority of humanity do not have the qualities needed to become full-time creators, and particularly creators who must toil away without any critical encouragement or support of patrons and colleagues.

Becoming a full-time creator is a fantasy even to the over-educated elites who promote the idea. If they were in fact the driven creative type, they wouldn't need a guaranteed income to fulfill their vision; they would already be doing it regardless of their circumstances.

There is one final failing in the fantasy of self-expression replacing work. The artists, writers and composers who succeeded in fulfilling their vision—whether they found a market for it or not—worked within communities of fellow creators, patrons, customers, gallery owners, etc. These peers provided encouragement, criticism, camaraderie, solace in the face of commercial or critical failure, inspiration, and often a place to work or gather. In other words, they worked in an ecosystem that enabled and nurtured their efforts.

Even largely solitary geniuses worked within networks of friends, fellow musicians and composers and patrons. The *cross fertilization of these overlapping networks* often fueled the artist's work.

- A violinist peer, for example, composed the cadenza for Beethoven's violin concerto.
- Mahler held an extremely demanding full-time job in the time he composed most of his symphonies.
- Goethe managed the estate and businesses of his patron for many years.
- Early jazz composers were by and large busy professional musicians, working and socializing with a wide circle of peers.

For such artists, their creative efforts *were* their work, and this work required the same dedication, effort, and networks of collaboration and support that all productive work requires.

To substitute for work, creative self-expression must be work.

Very few people have the self-directed drive, talent and enthusiasm needed to persevere despite little encouragement, and to assemble the networks of peers, customers, supporters and patrons that support artistic endeavor. The claim that creative self-expression will automatically substitute for work is not just a fantasy, it is a cruel fantasy, for it is unrealistic in the extreme.

The Fantasy of Paid Work from Creative Self-Expression

One offshoot of the myth that self-expression is a substitute for work is the idea that creative self-expression can generate a real income – that, thanks to the democratization of the arts and the marketplace, hundreds of thousands of newly unleashed creators could earn money on top of their monthly UBI benefit.

As noted earlier, recent events such as the democratization of the Web and the reduced cost of creative tools have resulted in an enormous expansion of creative products: novels, books, films, poems, videos, songs, etc., most of which have not been reviewed or curated.

This flood has fragmented the marketplace. For example, while a small number of musicians will still sell a million digital albums, most of the music sales are now spread over thousands of musicians and bands. This has created the false hope that an enormously expanded pool of musicians will be able to earn a living from small but dedicated fan bases nurtured on social media.

The Pareto Distribution, known as the 80/20 rule, sheds some light on the distribution of income to artists, writers, musicians, et al. Roughly 4% of creators garner 64% of all income (20% of 20% is 4 and 20% of 80% is 64, so 64/4 is a derivative of 80/20) while the other 96% share what's left in a distribution known as *the long tail*. In other words, those between 4% and 20% reap most of the remaining income, while the bottom 80% comprise the long tail of very modest to near-zero income.

It is difficult to gather meaningful statistics on this distribution. IRS statistics do not break down independent creators from other small enterprises, nor do they separate corporate employees such as editors and technical writers from independent writers. But evidence suggests that the income flowing to creators is even more skewed than 64/4: it may well be that the top 1% gathers 50% or more of the income, while the next 3% take a majority of what's left.

My analysis of IRS income data found that the number of people earning middle-class incomes from independently owned and operated sole proprietorships (excluding professionals such as doctors, accountants, engineers, attorneys, etc.) is extremely modest: perhaps 4 million workers out of a workforce of 150 million. Of these 4 million or so independents, how many earn a good living solely as creators? Again, there are no reliable statistics collected on independent (i.e. non-state supported) creators, but the number of self-supporting creators who earn a reliably middle-class income from their artistic output appears to be vanishingly small.

The IRS also reports royalty earnings, which typically flow to the owners of patents and creative content. Based on the IRS data, a relatively small handful of people receive the lion's share of royalties.

The number of artists, poets, musicians, writers, composers, etc. who make a middle-class living solely from the marketplace (i.e. no state or foundation grants, no corporate sponsorship, no financial support from wealthy patrons, no trust fund) is so small that it is effectively signal noise.

As the global audience becomes ever more accustomed to free music, free content, free videos, etc., the income flowing to creators is challenged not just by expanding competition but by a diminishing market for paid content. The music industry, for example, has shrunk from $17 billion annually to $7 billion.

The markets for creative content are a tiny sliver of the entire economy. The music industry's $7 billion and the publishing industry's $28 billion in revenues barely register in a U.S. GDP of $18 trillion. The entire film industry is around $30 billion, video-games $70 billion, and perhaps another $15 billion for the entire art market. The total of all these markets is less than 1% of the nation's economic activity. Note that these are revenues, not profits; the sums available to be paid as profits after all expenses have been deducted is an even tinier slice.

The idea that millions of newly freed-from-work people will find fulfillment via creative self-expression is as unfounded as the idea that millions of these new creators will earn significant sums for their creative endeavors. There is no evidence to support either claim.

The Fantasy of Subsidized Entrepreneurship

The other fantasy of the intellectual-technocrat elites is that UBI recipients will rush headlong into entrepreneurial ventures once the burdens of paid work are lifted from their shoulders. The assumption is that UBI recipients will in effect become subsidized entrepreneurs: once the risk of going hungry has been removed by Universal Basic Income, they will be chomping at the bit to start that business they always wanted to launch.

The claim that UBI will free recipients to become artists and entrepreneurs is an abstraction, an idealized dream with no connection to the lived-in world.

There are multiple fundamental flaws with the idea that UBI will subsidize entrepreneurship. I have already explained the critical role of capital and infrastructure of opportunity in *What Do the Wealthy Have that the Poor Don't Have?*

Let's start with a simple question: how many people do you personally know with a dependable source of unearned income (i.e. the equivalent of UBI) who have actually launched and grown a new enterprise over the long term?

The answer for the vast majority of us is *zero*. The number of people with a trust fund or equivalent income who undertake the complex and demanding task of starting an enterprise and making it a success is almost nil.

The reason is painfully obvious: why go to all that trouble and effort when your income is already guaranteed? At the first discouragement, the proto-entrepreneur gives up, deciding "this requires way too much effort, and I might end up making nothing, so why bother?"

Anecdotally, trust funders may dabble in starting an artsy (i.e. doomed to commercial failure) business, or invest in a friend's unrealistic venture. But entrepreneurship is incompatible with dabbling; entrepreneurship requires the utmost seriousness and commitment to commercial goals (i.e. making a profit). If that goal is lacking, losses mount and the enterprise fails.

The irony is that rather than expediting entrepreneurship, having a guaranteed income effectively kills the aspirational drive needed to succeed as an entrepreneur. The individual with a guaranteed income doesn't have the same *skin in the game* as the individual who must make the enterprise successful to earn a livelihood.

The fantasy also overlooks that entrepreneurs must exploit a profitable niche or they will exhaust their capital via losses and go out of business. The intellectuals and academics who are enamored with the fantasy that basic incomes will kindle an explosion of entrepreneurial activity have little actual entrepreneurial experience themselves. If they did, they would know that most profitable niches are already dominated by cartels or corporations that have developed specific skills to exploit those niches.

Enterprises can only survive if they turn a profit. Unprofitable enterprises incur losses that soon sink the enterprise and the entrepreneur.

Despite the hype about the wealth awaiting entrepreneurs, the reality is much more sobering. It is difficult to find a profitable niche that isn't already filled with competitors, and even more difficult to grow a business that makes a profit over the long-term.

Cheerleaders for the notion that UBI will release a flood of entrepreneurship overlook the reality that the majority of enterprises, large and small, require substantial investments of capital in all its forms: financial capital (i.e. cash and credit), human capital (the skills needed to launch and operate a business), social capital (the network of suppliers, customers, etc. needed to sustain the business) and the cultural and symbolic capital I described in the previous section. Simply being able to pay your household's basic living expenses does not automatically create the necessary capital for starting even a small enterprise, or give UBI recipients access to capital.

What advocates of the fantasy of subsidized entrepreneurship don't understand (or choose to ignore) is that isolated, atomized individuals with no access to the structures that enable and support new enterprises would have to create these complex networks of capital, skills and values without any *institutional memory* to aid them. This is, for the overwhelming percentage of humans, an impossibility. It isn't a matter of intelligence or effort or will; assembling all the forms of capital needed to create an *infrastructure of entrepreneurship and opportunity* is daunting, especially if there is no localized *institutional memory* to draw upon.

Institutional memory includes the experience of elders who led the way, well-worn channels of financing and guidance for new entrepreneurs, easily accessible expertise/talent and local government systems to enforce a level playing field and encourage new enterprises.

Just giving an individual enough cash to get by in a desert of no capital and no infrastructure of entrepreneurship is akin to dropping someone into the middle of a desert and expecting them to develop a thriving farm with no water, no well, no pump, no seeds, no fertilizer, no nearby experienced farmers to aid them, no networks of farm suppliers and produce customers, and no expertise in farming or the local ecosystem.

This is the hidden-in-plain-sight secret of Silicon Valley that many have tried to copy, generally with mixed success: entrepreneurship only becomes attainable in a sea of capital—not just financial capital, but human capital, mentors, and the symbolic and cultural capital which manifests as institutional memory of how to start businesses and guide them to sustainable success.

The privileged elites who promote this fantasy are like fish swimming in a sea of opportunity supported by a thriving ecosystem of capital; they don't see the wealth of capital around them, and so they assume everyone has the same opportunities they have.

Individuals don't create the social and economic structures they inhabit. As our example of the two young people with equal intelligence and education, the one who had access to *an infrastructure of entrepreneurism*—a virtual sea of capital to swim in—had far brighter prospects than the individual inhabiting a desert devoid of capital and opportunity.

Our goal should be to guarantee access to the interconnected networks of capital that makes up an *infrastructure of opportunity*. Without access to a supportive ecosystem of capital, entrepreneurial efforts will wither like seedlings deprived of water and nutrient-rich soil.

Proponents of guaranteed basic income implicitly assume that opportunities to start new profitable businesses will be so plentiful that millions of people just getting by on UBI will start new businesses. This overlooks the fact that the scarcity of profitable opportunities for those with little capital is what created the structural unemployment that UBI is designed to solve.

If opportunities to start new and profitable enterprises were indeed abundant for those with little access to capital, there would be no need for Universal Basic Income in the first place.

Advocates of the fantasy of UBI unleashing a tidal wave of entrepreneurial startups also overlook the sobering reality that many communities were never given much of a chance to develop an institutional memory of entrepreneurism. Independent enterprises were suppressed or starved due to ethnic bias, ethnic or geographical restrictions on ownership and loans.

In other cases, the community's institutional memory and local capital has been dissipated by dependence on global corporations or the government for employment.

Creating an institutional memory of entrepreneurism and the social and financial capital needed to nurture new enterprises requires a complex and self-sustaining infrastructure. UBI has no mechanism to create this infrastructure, and neither does the haphazard system of occasional state or foundation grants.

As I noted earlier, those supporting Universal Basic Income as a means of providing material security have the right goal, but this goal—

minimal material security—doesn't go far enough. While addressing the bottom rung of Maslow's human needs hierarchy—shelter, food, etc.— UBI does absolutely nothing to provide opportunities to fulfil our higher needs.

Stripped of idealistic fantasies, UBI is a quick-and-dirty means of placating an increasingly disenfranchised populace on the cheap, enabling the elites to hoard the capital, high-touch services and opportunities for meaningful work that are scarce and valuable.

Rather than creating a universal system for distributing the means to build capital and generate purposeful, fulfilling paid work, UBI reduces the disenfranchised to just-scraping-by consumers with little access to either capital or opportunity for what the elites themselves feel is their natural birthright: opportunities to forge fulfilling life's work, build capital, serve the community and gain access to high-touch services.

Unfortunately for UBI advocates, quick-and-dirty doesn't mean cheap, as all the breezy claims that UBI can be paid for by taxing the robots or the wealthy run aground on the shoals of the real world.

Universal Basic Income's Dependence on Maximizing Profits

There is nothing particularly natural about a system that encourages individuals to strip every last fruit from a tree and turn that one-time bounty into money that can be used to buy up all the other fruit trees in the area. Stripped of propaganda, this is the essence of any system based on maximizing private profit by any means available.

Once an individual owns all the productive trees in the area, he then distributes a bit of the harvest to each household that owns no productive assets at all. This distribution from those who own the productive wealth (the *means of production*) to those who own none is Universal Basic Income, shorn of its Orwellian idealization.

I have endeavored to reveal UBI's dependence on profits. Even a socialist nation that owns all its corporations must still maximize the profits earned by these state-owned enterprises to fund UBI.

I have also endeavored to explain that since UBI has no mechanism for creating capital, community or meaningful work, it simply formalizes the vast inequalities and impoverishment built into our current *maximize profits by any means available* Mode of Production.

The ontological problem with *maximizing profits by any means available* is that such a system makes no distinction between stripmining the seas to maximize profit and fishing in a sustainable fashion except in the profit potential of each. Since the wholesale stripmining of the seas maximizes profits in the present, that is what our system incentivizes. As noted earlier, there is zero profit to be had by restoring stripmined ecosystems, or in building social capital within a community shorn of productive capital.

Our current system also lacks any mechanism that distinguishes between speculative profits generated by *financialization*, i.e. the commoditization of once-safe assets via debt, leverage and securitization, and *profits generated by sustainable activity*.

Profit as *a measure of surplus generated by sustainable activity* has a positive role in human life. This is the core idea behind *free markets* as described by Adam Smith: productive activity guided by the *invisible hand* of consumer demand and producers' supply.

But our current Mode of Production has no mechanism for making such distinctions because all that matters is maximizing profit by any means available, regardless of the negative consequences to those not reaping the profits.

Facebook offers a contemporary example. Facebook and other social media are free services. How do they pay for the immense costs of operating their services and reap a profit for shareholders? They sell advertisements and paid content. Given the inner logic of our Mode of Production, Facebook's core *ontological imperative* is to maximize profit by whatever means are available. (This would be still be the case even if Facebook were owned by a socialist state.)

How can Facebook maximize profits? The answer is to replace passive metrics of page views, etc., with *engagement*, that is, measures of users' responses to adverts and paid content. The greater the emotional impact of the adverts/paid content, the higher the user engagement. This greater engagement increases the value of the adverts/paid content and thus profits.

Since users are extremely *engaged* when responding to paid content that outrages them, whatever content maximizes users' emotional response is also the most profitable content. The inner logic of this revenue source incentivizes Facebook to direct content that is likely to stimulate some emotional response—whether the reaction is positive or negative makes no difference.

Since Facebook collects comprehensive data on each user, the company can sell highly targeted adverts and paid content, so-called "dark ads" that are only visible to select audiences known only to the advertiser and Facebook.

The inner logic of maximizing profit in an advert-revenue model leads to this inner logic of maximizing emotional responses by any means available: fake news, hysterically exaggerated claims, and so on— whatever stimulates *engagement*, no matter how perverse or destructive, pushes profits higher.

UBI advocates view the profits needed to fund UBI in a calculatedly sanitized way, as if profits are not just inevitable, they're also magically clean and abundant: robots and software will do the dirty work, immense profits are generated by some sort of alchemy, and these profits are siphoned off to fund UBI.

The reality is considerably messier. Profits are not inevitable, nor are they clean in the current Mode of production, which extracts the vast majority of its profits by exploiting natural capital (our planet) and labor, and promoting wasteful, unsustainable overconsumption in a globalized *Landfill Economy*.

The uncomfortable reality is that Universal Basic Income is the last gasp of a dying system, a system based on the unsustainable exploitation of the planet and its inhabitants to fuel debt-financed overconsumption and profiteering.

Meaningful Work Is Wealth; the Demand for High-Touch Work

This analysis leads to a startling conclusion: *wealth isn't a life of 100% leisure in a consumer-centric society; wealth is the opportunity for purposeful, socially valued, meaningful work that builds capital in all its forms.* Wealth isn't only what work earns; *meaningful work itself is wealth* as it provides what every human needs: a source of purpose, pride and self-worth; a means of acquiring capital; a positive social role, i.e. a means to be needed by others; self-fulfillment / self-actualization; to contribute to a purpose greater than oneself and the opportunity make a positive difference in others' lives.

This is the exact opposite of what Universal Basic Income assumes is wealth.

UBI assumes that human labor will inexorably be replaced by robots and software, and since humans will not have any work to do, they won't have an income, either. This assumption is false, as it fails to distinguish between the low-touch commoditized work that lends itself to automation *and high-touch work whose value is social and thus incapable of being automated.*

While UBI advocates write off everyone who isn't in the ranks of the multi-skilled elites whose work doesn't lend itself to automation, they ignore the many lower-skilled high-touch tasks that communities need, and the many forms of high-touch work in which humans use technology as collaborative tools.

The advocates of UBI assume a bleak future in which there is little need for human labor and thus little opportunity for meaningful work. The reality is that there is an essentially insatiable need for high-touch services and the social value they generate that by definition cannot be replaced by robots.

Indeed, if we compare the lives of the elite class and the bottom 90%, what's most striking is the elite class has ready access to high-touch services, from dog walkers to doctors: in-home care for elders, attorneys, personal trainers, private lessons for the children, etc. The value in all these high-touch services is that they are individualized, non-tradable, non-commoditized, and performed by a human being. Meanwhile, most of these high-touch services are beyond the financial reach of the bottom 90% slated for the impoverishment of UBI.

Even more striking is the relationship each class has with the low-touch automated services that are supposed to replace the high-touch services enjoyed by the elite class: the elite class designs and manages the commoditized, automated services for the bottom 90% but avoids any interaction with their own handiwork.

The elite class implicitly benefits from a scarcity of meaningful work, as this enables them to hire high-touch human-provided services on the cheap due to the oversupply of conventional labor.

I hope you see the outlines of a much more just and equitable alternative system, a system that guarantees not the institutionalized impoverishment of UBI but access for all to the high-touch services and meaningful the elites expect as a birthright.

IV. The Structural Failure of the Current Mode of Production

What's Broken?

As noted earlier, value flows to what's scarce and in demand. One way to answer the question, *what's scarce?* is to ask, *what's broken?*, for solutions to what's broken are obviously scarce, or the problem wouldn't exist.

What's broken in our world is the entire *Mode of Production*: the way we exploit and extract resources, the way we invest capital and labor to transform those resources into products, and the way we distribute those resources and products—that is, the way we extract our planet's natural capital and distribute income, wealth and capital.

What's broken is the health of the soil depleted by factory farming. What's scarce is healthy soil, healthy habitats and sustainable ways of farming that don't deplete or poison the soil. Rigging a tractor to be self-driving (i.e. automation) won't solve any of these problems. Eliminating the human work force that once harvested crops won't fix what's broken in our Mode of Production, our economy or our society.

You see the core problem. Our *Mode of Production* is based on a simple but false premise: *whatever maximizes profits will magically fill all scarcities and fix our most pressing problems.* This leads to the core assumption of robots and automation, which is that *the problem is human labor costs too much, so eliminating human labor will solve our core problem.*

In other words, the problem with human labor is its cost: if we could eliminate that cost, prices could fall and profits could rise: the idealized perfection of a profit-maximizing system.

But replacing all the human labor in factory farming won't restore depleted soil, because restoring depleted soil is inherently unprofitable.

Replacing the human crews of fishing fleets stripmining the seas won't restore depleted wild fisheries.

In other words, automating human labor doesn't fix what's broken. What's broken is our entire *Mode of Production* that plows under all the unprofitable systems needed to sustain ecosystems, localized production and social cohesion.

From the perspective of what's broken, robots and automation only speed up the pillaging of the planet in service of maximizing profits in the here and now, regardless of the cost to the Commons or future generations.

How we decide to invest capital is also broken. Since over-investment and overcapacity are intrinsic dynamics of the current Mode of Production, the profitability of commoditized robots and other tools of automation quickly falls near zero, since there is little to no scarcity value in commoditized output, or indeed, in conventional capital itself. Since we only invest in what's profitable, scarcities that aren't profitable to fill are left unmet.

The way we produce goods is broken, as the goal of maximizing profits is best served by planned obsolescence, forcing consumers to replace products often, and designing the products not just to fail but to be impossible to repair. This inner logic of our Mode of Production has rendered the global economy a *Landfill Economy*, in which every product is thrown away after a brief service.

There is no profit to be had in repairing or collecting the vast outpouring of goods tossed aside in the *Landfill Economy*, and so a slowly swirling gyre of plastic trash the size of Texas now occupies the central Pacific, and remote islands are covered in plastic water bottles and other debris of maximizing profit by any means available.

Our conceptual grasp of work is broken, as neither the market focused on maximizing profit nor the centralized state can differentiate between BS work and meaningful work. Our economic understanding of the value of work is equally broken, as profitability is the sole director of what work is paid in the private sector.

The incentive structure is also broken, as the incentive to maximize profits by any means available is intrinsically short-sighted and destructive of all that is unprofitable: restoring stripmined environments, nurturing community social capital and so on. The central state's incentive structure is equally perverse, as dependence on the state cripples communities while rendering the populace compliant to the state elites' predations.

What's Scarce?

Our conceptual grasp of scarcity is also broken, as scarcities that can't profitably be filled by the market or state don't register in the current Mode of Production. The scarcity of socially cohesive communities, for example, simply isn't recognized in the current system; if a wasteland of dollar stores and fast-food outlets is profitable (i.e. there is adequate consumption of corporate goods and services funded by social welfare such as UBI), our Mode of Production has *no mechanism to recognize* the scarcity of social cohesion in the community, much less address it.

Since *we optimize what we measure and we measure what the system values*, and the current Mode of Production measures profit and consumption, a community stripped of capital, productive capacity and social cohesion has acceptable metrics as long as consumption and profits are satisfactory.

The great irony in this systemic disavowal of scarcities that cannot be profitably met by commoditized production is that since value flows to what's scarce, *what cannot be purchased on the global market or provided by the state has the highest value.*

Examples of what cannot be bought on the global marketplace include: positive social roles; a collective memory of how to get things done using local labor, resources and capital; meaningful work; functioning community economies, and social cohesion.

In other words, all these foundations of human fulfillment are considered valueless in the current Mode of Production because they can't be commoditized, financialized or otherwise rendered profitable to mobile global capital. Yet their scarcity in a world overflowing with commoditized goods and services makes them valuable in ways the current system can't even recognize, much less value or measure.

In the conventional view, what's scarce is high yield on capital and opportunities for vast profits. But what's actually scarce, but unrecognized as a scarcity, is *affordable high-touch services, infrastructures of opportunity, mechanisms to fill local scarcities that aren't profitable to fill, community cohesion, well-maintained public spaces* and *permanent, paid meaningful work.*

What's scarce are ways of living that actually fix what's broken, ways of living that are sustainable over the long haul and that restore the foundations of human happiness and social cohesion: meaningful work and positive social roles embedded in localized, community production.

The Current System Has No Mechanism to Differentiate Fundamentally Different Things

If we had to summarize the key conceptual failing of the current Mode of Production, it would be: *the current system has no mechanism to differentiate between fundamentally different things.*

The highest and best use of capital and labor in the current system is to maximize profit by whatever means are available. But there is no mechanism to differentiate between speculative gains reaped by financialization, a process that generates no jobs, goods or services, and an investment of capital and labor that generates new jobs, goods or services. The first is exploitive, the second is productive.

Clearly, these are *fundamentally different things.*

The system has no mechanism to differentiate between sustainable harvesting of ecosystems and stripmining those ecosystems. Yet these are *fundamentally different things.*

The system has no mechanism to differentiate between serfdom and wages that generate financial security. Yet these are *fundamentally different things.*

Some work is BS work, understood by everyone involved to be unnecessary outside the perverse demands of centralized hierarchies. Other work is needed and meaningful to everyone involved. The two kinds of work are fundamentally different, but the system has no mechanism to differentiate these fundamentally different things.

In our current system, BS work is paid while a vast spectrum of meaningful work is unpaid because it isn't profitable or paid by the central state.

A community that retains a collective memory of how to work together to get important projects done is fundamentally different from a community shorn of this collective reservoir of social capital. There is no mechanism in the current Mode of Production to differentiate between these fundamentally different things.

Universal Basic Income is widely viewed as the ideal solution in the current Mode of Production because the system has no mechanism to differentiate between a society stripped of positive social roles and one with an abundance of positive social roles. Yet these are *fundamentally different societies.*

The current system only values and thus only measures what can be priced in the global marketplace. It presumes that maximizing profit by expanding consumption will fill all scarcities. In other words, communities and societies that are organized around expanding consumption and profit will also maximize happiness because happiness is presumed to be a function of consumerist desires and needs—i.e. scarcities—being filled.

This system has no mechanism to differentiate between a consumerist society that has been stripped of the foundations of human happiness—that is, a society of misery in which *everything that is truly valuable is scarce* because it can't be profitably commoditized—and a society with an abundance of the sources of human happiness.

The Wrong Unit Size and the Wrong Structure

Not only does the current Mode of Production lack any mechanism to differentiate between fundamentally different things, the two intertwined systems that make up the Mode of Production—the profit-maximizing marketplace and the central state—are the *wrong unit size and the wrong structure.*

Scarcities in communities are presumed to be scarcities of commoditized goods and services that can be filled by global corporations and funded by central state programs such as UBI. But what about scarcities of social cohesion, positive social roles, resilience, and the ability to work together without being commandeered by corporate or state hierarchies?

The scarcities that can be filled by global corporations and the central state are fundamentally different from the scarcities listed above. The core failure to differentiate between fundamentally different types of scarcities is not just a failure of the profit-maximizing marketplace; it is the direct result of the marketplace and the central state that manages the marketplace being the *wrong unit size* and *the wrong structure.*

Put another way: how can a global system of production and a vast central state grasp the complexities of scarcities within localized communities? Centralized hierarchies of concentrated power are simply the wrong unit size for filling local scarcities. Localized, decentralized structures are the only unit size that can recognize and address the scarcities that can't be filled on the global marketplace.

The central state is the perfect unit size to create dependence on the state at the expense of community resilience, self-sufficiency and capital accumulation. Universal Basic Income is the perfection of dependence on the central state at the expense of local governance, capital and control of local resources.

The central bank/private bank system is also the wrong unit size and structure, as its monopoly over the creation and distribution of new credit/money insures an incestuous concentration of wealth and power in the privileged few with access to the new credit/money. There is no other possible output of this structure other than the extreme concentration of wealth and power in the hands of the few at the expense of the 99.9% with no equivalent access to the central bank spigots of *nearly free money.*

These corporate, banking and state structures are *the wrong structure* because their structure concentrates power and wealth in the apex of the wealth-power pyramid, enriching the few by stripmining the many. Concentrated wealth buys political power which accumulates wealth which buys more power. The only possible output of this self-reinforcing concentration of wealth and power is rising wealth-power inequality.

Centralized hierarchies of concentrated power are also the *wrong structure* because they are Procrustean Beds that cut or stretch everything to a form the hierarchies recognize. And what they recognize is a global marketplace of consumer goods and services overseen by a central state and funded by credit created by a central bank.

Everything outside this structure doesn't exist. You can't order social cohesion through Amazon, or lobby for a law mandating social cohesion.

The core concept here is *what cannot be purchased on the global market or provided by the state is scarce because it cannot be commoditized, and thus has the highest value.*

The Internal Logic of the Current Mode of Production

Why can't we create more paid work and more profits in the current system? Why can't the state tax these profits to pay millions of unemployed people Universal Basic Income as a permanent entitlement? Advocates of the current Mode of Production fail to grasp the self-destructive logic of the current system.

This internal logic of the current Mode of Production is straightforward: an infinite expansion of credit-money funds an infinite expansion of consumption that then powers an infinite expansion of production which generates an infinite expansion of profits which then funds Universal Basic Income, which is the teleological (i.e. ultimate) end-state of the system's internal logic: infinite consumption funded by an infinite expansion of credit funded by taxing an infinite expansion of profits.

The social desert of atomized individuals purchasing commoditized goods and services from global corporations is deemed the perfection of human happiness.

This internal logic has no use for positive social roles, meaningful work, social cohesion and functioning communities; these foundations of human happiness are implicitly assumed to magically arise out of the infinite expansion of credit, consumption, production, profits and state-controlled distribution of UBI.

But these foundations don't magically arise out of the infinite expansion of credit, consumption and tax revenues. *The Mode of Production must yield these foundations as a direct output.* In the current system, these foundations aren't recognized, measured or valued; they simply don't exist within our infinite expansion of finance-based consumption.

As noted in the previous section, the current Mode of Production has three conceptual flaws:

The current system has no mechanism to differentiate between fundamentally different things.

The profit-maximizing marketplace and the central state are the wrong unit size and the wrong structure; these structures institutionalize perverse incentives and concentrate wealth and power in the hands of the few at the expense of the many.

The highest-value scarcities—those that cannot be filled by the state or by purchasing commoditized goods and services on the global market—are not recognized or valued.

Let's examine the internal logic of the current Mode of Production's core dynamics:

Infinite expansion of consumption on a finite planet. The internal logic of the current system requires infinite expansion of everything, including extraction of resources and the production of more goods fashioned from those resources. If consumption falls, credit falls, profit falls, tax revenues fall and the system collapses under the weight of debts and obligations that cannot be met.

Maximizing profit by any means available. The logic of profit maximization is intolerant of niceties such as ethics, conservation of unprofitable resources, etc. Any owner or manager who reduces profits in pursuit of unprofitable niceties will be sacked or driven out of business by competitors with no such costs. Capital will abandon any venture that reduces profits for any reason, ethical or otherwise.

If competitors are skirting regulations to boost profits, any enterprise wishing to survive must follow suit lest its profits falter. If subverting democracy via buying political influence increases profits, the logic of maximizing profits demands enterprises subvert democracy. The key phrase is *by any means available*. The internal logic does not allow exceptions. All private costs must be ruthlessly externalized (dumped on the Commons, Nature or local communities) lest competitors who have externalized their costs drive those absorbing these costs into the ground.

Planned obsolescence and waste is more profitable than DeGrowth/consuming less. Durable products that don't require replacement are profit-killers. Services that don't need to be renewed are profit-killers. Since maximizing profits by any means available is the Prime Directive of the system, the internal logic demand the optimization of planned obsolescence and waste.

Systemic dependence on debt to fund consumption. Since savings—what's left after all expenses are deducted from income—cannot possibly fund the rapid expansion of consumption required to sustain the current system, the existing Mode of Production is completely dependent on the rapid expansion of credit to fund private and public consumption. Were the system's issuance of credit to freeze up, consumption and state spending would plummet, triggering a depression.

Over-investment, over-capacity and commoditization destroy profits, even as the internal logic of maximizing profits demands over-investment and commoditization as the means of expanding market share and sales.

Money is created and distributed at the top of the wealth-power pyramid; interest flows from debtors to the few at the top. The only possible output of this system is rising wealth and income inequality. As I have described many times in previous books, money in the current system is borrowed into existence by central banks that create currency out of thin air to buy interest-bearing bonds with the new money, or it's borrowed into existence by private banks that create new money via the origination of new loans.

The internal logic of this system is two-fold: all new money is credit-money and thus interest must be paid by borrowers, and all new money is created and distributed by banks.

The internal logic demands that interest sluices income from borrowers to the lenders. Over time, interest payments impoverish borrowers and enrich lenders and those who own the debt-based assets, i.e. the financial elite.

The internal logic of lending money into existence is that the new money is most profitably and safely lent to those with abundant collateral and income to support the new loan, i.e. the wealthy. The wealthy thus have the credit needed to outbid everyone else for productive (income-producing) assets: housing, stocks, mines, bonds, mortgage-backed securities, and so on.

The only possible result of these dynamics is that the productive capital of the bottom 90% is replaced with debt as the capital and income of the bottom 90% flow to the top 10%. Since the rewards of financialization—the financial legerdemain of leverage, securitization and the asymmetrical concentration of speculative expertise—flow to the top .1% of households, the immense profits created by financial engineering and speculation are distributed in a power-law curve, with the vast majority of these profits flowing to the top .1%.

It's important to note that financialization doesn't expand the pool of goods, services or jobs; this extraction of financial profits generates no new productivity, goods, services or jobs. Financialization is intrinsically predatory and parasitic.

These dynamics have only one output: the impoverishment of borrowers and the expansion of the wealth and income of the financial elite. There is no other possible output of this system.

Capital flows to whatever maximizes profits. There is no mechanism in the current Mode of Production to measure the productive investment of capital other than the maximization of profit. As Marx observed, the most profitable arrangement is a privately owned monopoly enforced by a central state. The internal logic of monopoly is to destroy competition and transparency, and secure political protection from the government.

The most profitable private arrangement is to buy the complicity of the central state. The internal logic of a system in which the state controls the marketplace is for private-sector wealth to buy whatever political influence is necessary to protect private profits and socialize any losses, i.e. transfer losses incurred by private-sector banks to the taxpayers. The only possible output of this logic is a *pay-to-play form of democracy in which wealth casts the only votes that count.*

In other words, the current Mode of Production is intrinsically destructive to democracy.

Consumption, income and profits must expand at rates higher than the expansion of interest payments. As noted, all new money in the current system accrues interest. If the income of borrowers doesn't outpace the expansion of debt and interest, then the only possible result is default and insolvency, that is, borrowers can no longer pay the interest due as the interest has risen while their income has stagnated.

Since debt is an asset, default destroys debt-based wealth such as bonds and mortgage-backed securities.

Financial capital is mobile. Financial capital is free to flow through the global economy, seeking the lowest-risk, highest yield investments. The internal logic of mobile capital is to get in, maximize profits and then get out before profit-killing factors such as the costs of environmental degradation (often referred to as *external costs*) or demands for higher wages arise.

The internal logic of mobile capital ignores whatever damage is left behind by the exploitation of resources, markets and people. The only directive of capital is to maximize profits and grow capital; nothing else matters. Whatever impinges on this directive is jettisoned, abandoned, crushed or bribed into complicity.

There is no mechanism to differentiate between capital that is embedded in a community for the long-term and mobile capital that financializes the local assets into securities that can be sold on the global marketplace, destroys local production by importing cheaper goods and services, indebts the residents by expanding credit and then leaves once profits have been maximized via the sale of the newly commoditized assets on the global market.

Universal Basic Income is the ideal end-state of the system's internal logic. UBI is the perfect end-state for those holding the wealth and power in the current Mode of Production, for UBI funds the consumption of the masses, effectively neutering them politically, while concentrating wealth and power in the entitled elite class that hoards what's scarce and valuable: capital, opportunities to accumulate capital and meaningful, rewarding work.

We can now understand why the current Mode of Production is self-destructive; the internal logic generates incentives that destroy the planet's natural capital and the pyramid of debt that funds the system's over-capacity and over-consumption.

To paraphrase Immanuel Wallerstein, *capitalism is no longer attractive to capitalists*. To the degree that state-owned enterprises must be profitable to fund the state, we can also say that *socialism is no longer attractive to socialists*.

The False Promise of Ever-Expanding Profits via Automation

The core assumption of the current Mode of Production is that profits will expand as automation replaces human labor. The core assumption of advocates of Universal Basic Income is that these ever-expanding profits will effortlessly fund UBI. Both assumptions are profoundly false.

We've already covered in the previous section on the economics of automation that robots will only perform profitable work, but that is not the only dynamic impacting profits and automation. An example will help explain how the internal logic of our Mode of Production leads to diminishing returns on both capital and labor.

The Impact of Supply and Demand on Profit

Let's consider bottles of fresh water. In the summer, the beach is hot and there will be demand from people who have become thirsty. If there is no public fountain, fresh water has a high utility value, and cold fresh water will be even more desirable on hot days.

How can a vendor of bottled fresh water secure high profits? Let's start by considering the impact of wide-open competition on the source of profit, scarcity.

The first vendor on the beach quickly sells all his cold water, and rushes back to get more. This time he raises the price. He continues to do this until customers start balking at the price. This the highest price the market can bear.

However, it doesn't take long for other vendors to notice the profit potential, and soon there are dozens of vendors selling the same cold water bottles.

The Impact of Competition on Profit

Wide open competition destroys profits as the horde of vendors must cut prices to keep making sales. If there are dozens of vendors on the beach selling the same chilled bottles of fresh water, the only way to entice a potential customer to buy from you rather than a competitor is to lower the price below that being asked by competitors.

If there is competition, there's no *pricing power*, which is the ability to raise prices high enough to generate profits. Why would a customer pay extra for the same bottle of water she can buy for less from another vendor?

The first vendor may have reaped 50 cents of profit per bottle early on, but with dozens of vendors selling the same water, soon the profit plummets to 5 cents per bottle for each of the vendors.

There are two other dynamics to consider: *demand* and *commoditization*.

- Demand is *elastic*, meaning that it will rise on hotter days and decline on overcast days. And there are limits on demand: if the vendors ask too high a price, people will forego satisfying their thirst and wait to get home to drink water. Once people are no longer thirsty, their desire for more bottles of water plummets. At this point, cutting the price further won't generate more sales, since the demand has been met.

- If all the bottles of water being offered by vendors are interchangeable, the bottled water is a *commodity*. When there is no discernable difference between brands, there is no pricing power.

Four Ways to Generate High Profits

There are four basic ways a vendor can gain pricing power and raise his prices enough to generate high profits. The vendor can:

1. Differentiate his product so it's no longer a commodity
2. Increase demand for the product
3. Lower production costs
4. Enforce a monopoly (that is, eliminate competition so he is the only vendor selling bottled water on the beach)

To differentiate his product, a vendor might start selling flavored water, or carbonated water that he can claim is superior in quality to every other vendor's commoditized water. This strategy is often initially successful, but other vendors will quickly copy the strategy, and the innovator's pricing power will soon disappear as other vendors also start selling flavored and carbonated water.

The second strategy is to increase demand. The innovative vendor might freeze his water into a slush, add coloring and sugar, and offer a festive slush drink. Since this has appeal above and beyond slaking thirst, this vendor can satisfy a demand which previously didn't exist. However, this innovation is also quickly copied, and the initial pricing power melts away.

You see the problem here: every innovation is quickly copied, i.e. *commoditized*, and so the only way for any vendor to maintain pricing power via innovation is to keep innovating as competitors turn every previous innovation into a commodity, at which point the pricing power for every vendor declines rapidly.

The third strategy is to lower the *cost of production*, which for the vendors is the cost of the bottled water and the time/transport costs of getting the bottles to the beach.

A savvy vendor might decide to try filtering and bottling his own product, cutting out the bottler and the wholesaler. He may find that this does lower his costs, but only if he manages an *economy of scale*. This term describes the cost advantages of increasing production:

- If the vendor filters and fills 100 bottles of water by hand, he might find his unit cost is actually higher than the wholesale price of the commodity bottles, due to the time it takes to fill and cap the bottles by hand.
- If the vendor can buy a second-hand machine that automates the filtering, filling and capping, the per-unit cost drops dramatically. With the machine, he can produce 1,000 bottles in the same time it took to fill and cap 100 bottles by hand.

In the second case, the machine is a form of *capital*, that is, an asset that dramatically increases production and reduces the per-unit labor cost. If we look at how many bottles the vendor can fill and cap in a day, his *productivity* has increased ten-fold: he can produce ten times more output than he did when working without the machine. The investment in capital has generated an enormous increase in productivity.

However, it takes money to buy the machine, and there are only two ways to get that large sum: one is to save up over time, and the other is to borrow the money, i.e. *credit*.

Since profit margins on the beach are low because of the wide-open competition, it's difficult for any individual vendor to save up enough cash to buy the bottling machine. The solution is to either borrow the money, or assemble the savings of a group of vendors and share the profits earned by lowering production costs.

The Impact of Credit on Profit

Why share profits with others if you can secure them all for yourself with a low-cost loan? Still using our beach/water example, the highest profit potential is for one vendor to buy a bottling machine at a low rate of interest. Interest is the cost of borrowing money, and over time, this cost can either lock in profitably low production costs if it's low...or consume all the potential profits if it's high.

Let's compare three vendors, each with the same idea of buying a bottling machine.

1. The first one can't find any bank or lender to loan him the money; he's told he is a poor credit risk because he doesn't have much income or collateral (tangible assets that could be sold to pay off the loan if he stops making payments).
2. The second vendor finds a local businessman who will loan him the money, but the interest rate is so high that he won't make any money even with the machine lowering his cost of production.
3. The third vendor has the privilege of access to low-interest credit. He can borrow the money at a low rate of interest even with his modest income and lack of collateral.

Note that this last lucky vendor had the same original idea as the other vendors. The only difference between the three is the access to low-cost credit.

This example reveals the essential role of low-cost credit: the vendor with access to low-cost credit can lock in lower production costs and high profits by buying the machine with credit.

In effect, access to low-cost credit establishes a *monopoly*: since the other vendors don't have the advantage of lower production costs, they cannot match the machine-owning vendor's price cuts. He can cut prices below what the other vendors pay the wholesaler for their bottles, driving them out of business. No one can afford to sell a bottle of water for less than it costs to buy from the wholesaler.

Access to low-cost credit enables one vendor to eliminate all his competition and establish a monopoly on the beach.

The Impact of Monopolies on Profit

The surest way to secure high profits is to maintain a *monopoly*. If one vendor can prohibit all other vendors from selling on the beach, or drive them out of business, he can charge whatever the market will bear—in other words, a price that's high enough to generate a nice profit but not so high people will forego quenching their thirst by waiting to go home to drink water.

Monopoly enforces an *artificial scarcity*. In a monopoly, customers on the beach can only buy water from one vendor. This artificial scarcity gives the one vendor pricing power that would not exist in wide-open competition.

We've already covered the role of credit in establishing a monopoly, but there are many other, more nefarious ways to enforce a monopoly. One vendor might bribe the wholesaler to charge his competitors a higher price than he gets from the wholesaler. Or he might bribe the beachside resort or local government authorities to ban all the other water vendors from the beach.

This reveals the essential role of *authority* in enforcing monopoly. If a vendor can't create a monopoly by lowering his cost of production, he can pay the authorities a slice of his profits to limit competition. (In areas with weak government authority, a vendor could pay a gang of thugs to terrorize competing vendors. This is for-hire private authority, enforced by the threat of violence.)

One profitable variation of monopoly is a *cartel*, which is a formal or informal agreement between enterprises in the same market to fix prices at levels that guarantee substantial profits for all members of the cartel.

Guilds perform the same function. If customers can only buy from a member of the guild (a limit that must be enforced by a government), the guild can enforce an artificial scarcity by limiting the number of guild members.

Returning to our beach/water example again, suppose three of the vendors manage to lower their cost of production to the point where they can drive all other vendors out of business. Rather than compete with each other by lowering prices (a competition that slashes the profits of everyone), these three can then agree to keep prices high enough that all three reap substantial profits.

Let's review what we've learned about profit.

Profits flow reliably to monopolies, cartels and guilds that limit competition by enforcing an artificial scarcity. This is the core relationship of competition, monopoly and profit.

There are two ways to achieve sustainable monopoly:

(1) Access to low-cost credit that other competitors do not have, credit which enables the reduction of production costs via economies of scale, and
(2) The cooperation of authority, which limits competition via regulations enforced by penalties. These are the core relationships between credit, authority, monopoly and profit.

The Impact of Labor and Production Costs on Profit

The final relationships to explore are those between labor (paid work), production costs and profit.

As we've seen earlier, if competition between vendors selling water on the beach is wide open, the profits available to each vendor are very low. Each vendor is lucky to sell enough low-profit bottles of water to eke out a modest daily wage.

A vendor might want to hire someone to help him sell more bottles, but with profit margins razor-thin, there isn't enough profit to pay the worker and leave a profit for the employer-vendor.

In wide-open competition, profits are so low that the vendors have trouble eking out a wage. There simply isn't enough profit to hire any employees.

Remember our lucky vendor with access to low-cost credit who buys the bottling machine? Unfortunately, now he has another problem:

- If he tends the machine all day, he has no time to go to the beach to sell his product.
- If he sells all day, he can't operate the bottling machine.

The obvious solution is to hire someone to either tend the machine or sell the product on the beach.

The canny vendor makes a calculation: where is he most productive, tending the machine or selling on the beach? Which task is preferable?

Suppose he decides to tend the machine and hire someone to sell. He's observed all the other vendors, and noted who tends to sell the most bottles by day's end. The vendor approaches one of these successful sellers and makes an offer: "You only make 5 cents per bottle now, and can't make more because others will undercut your price. I'll give you 10 cents per bottle to sell my product."

Due to his lower cost of production, the machine-owning (i.e. capital-owning) vendor can pay 5 cents more per bottle and still reap more profit than the other vendors.

Over time, more independent vendors become employees of the capital-owning vendor because they make more working for him.

As his staff of vendors grows, the employer realizes there isn't that much difference in the work done by his beach vendors. Some sell more than others due to their marketing skills and effort, and to keep these more productive workers, he offers them a base salary and commission on the bottles they sell.

What he really needs, though, is a mechanic to maintain his bottling machine, which keeps breaking down. If he can't find someone with specific experience maintaining this machine, he can train someone with general mechanical knowledge.

He finds such a mechanic, and discovers to his dismay the mechanic is going to cost him four times as much per day as his sales employees. The mechanic can charge more for his labor because his skillset is scarce; mechanics are few and far between.

Skills that are scarce generate high wages. If the work is simple enough to be done by almost anyone, the value of that work will be low because almost everyone has the skills needed to do the work.

On the other hand, if there is only one welder in town, and you need a broken part welded, the welder can charge a premium because his service is scarce. Competing welders may work in nearby towns, but if the time and expense of traveling to another town is prohibitive, the local welder's scarcity value remains high (assuming the quality of his work is equal to outside welders).

Note that welding is not a skill most people can pick up in a few hours; it also requires costly tools (e.g. the welding torch). The high skills and capital required to perform welding are both *barriers to entry*. The higher the barriers to entry, the more defendable the scarcity becomes.

Labor scarcities are dynamic. If graduates with Master's level business degrees are scarce and command high wages as a result, more students will opt to spend the time and money to obtain an MBA. If the demand for MBAs slows and/or the supply soars, the scarcity value of an MBA declines accordingly.

Even though our water vendor is paying the mechanic a high wage, this makes financial sense because now he loses less production time to mechanical problems.

Our vendor is making enough profit now that he has *surplus income*. He can afford to pay off his loan, or buy a faster bottling machine. He can also afford to pay for household services that were previously unpaid: he can hire someone to cook his family's meals, care for his children, and so on, freeing family members who had been performing those services without pay.

The key point here is the vendor could only hire people when he generated enough profit to do so. This is why *the source of paid work is profit*. At first, the vendor could only hire production workers, but as his profits expanded, he had enough income to start paying for non-business services that were previously unpaid.

Now that he is making substantial profits, he must pay taxes to the local government. This increased government revenue stream enables the local government to hire another employee. Although the government is the employer, the means to pay this new government employee comes from the vendor's profits.

Back when the competing vendors barely eked out a modest wage, nobody made enough of a profit to pay much tax: low profits equal scarce paid work and minimal taxes paid.

The Impact of Automation on Profits

Let's assume at this point disaster strikes. A large corporation sniffs out the profit potential of selling water on the beach and installs an automated vending machine that distributes cold bottles of water at a cost far below the production costs of our vendor. The corporation's entire bottling process is automated, and it can service dozens of vending machines with just a few employees.

In effect, the corporation has eliminated the sales staff by incentivizing the customers to get their own water bottles. This is the same dynamic behind self-checkout: customers perform work that was previously performed by paid staff.

The corporation's key competitive advantage is its access to cheap credit. The corporation can borrow the money needed to buy (or manufacture) the automated vending machines at rates of interest far lower than those available to our local vendor.

At first, our vendor keeps his sales employees on salary, but the corporate vending machines take away so much of his sales that he's losing money every day. Paying his employees to perform work that is no longer profitable will quickly drain his cash, leaving him no choice but either close his business or lay off his employees.

Our vendor naturally considers buying his own automated vending machine. He will have to borrow a lot of money to buy it, and the cost of borrowing this large sum reduces his profits to a razor thin slice. To survive, he fires all his household employees, goes into debt to buy the vending machine and stocks it himself.

This is not the end of the process of automation and cheap credit. Another global corporation has even cheaper credit costs, and an even lower cost automated supply chain, and so they install a vending a machine that lowers the price of bottled water below our local vendor's costs of production.

One of the new competitor's cost advantages is that it no longer pays employees to fill its vending machines; it hires informal workers on the *gig economy model* in which employers and free-lance workers each bid on an auction marketplace.

So the local vendor sells his vending machine and is reduced to bidding on the occasional job of filling the corporate vending machines, while the initial corporation is driven to follow the new competitor's model of reducing costs by using the gig economy model of obtaining the lowest possible cost labor.

Profit margins have been reduced to very low levels by cheap credit, automation and competition.

Note that automation didn't generate higher profits; it dramatically reduced them, as anyone with access to low-cost credit could buy the exact same vending machine. Automation eliminated a wide variety of paid work, but it didn't generate high profits. Whatever profits the global corporations reap from their vending machines—a modest sum from each machine, aggregated by *economies of scale*--flow back to corporate headquarters and distant owners; the profits and wages of our local vendor and his employees vanish.

As a result, local government tax revenues also plummet; there are fewer wage earners and less profits to tax.

The Impact of Government Ownership

Let's consider another scenario. The local government decides to ban all private vendors and vending machines on the beach and become the sole supplier of cold water on the beach. It also increases the price of the water sold to support the higher wages it pays its employees.

The State (i.e. the government) is by definition a monopoly, as it maintains a monopoly on imposing taxes and enforcing regulations.

But while the State can limit competition by imposing a monopoly, it cannot control demand. If the price of the bottled water supplied by the State rises high enough, beachgoers will forego buying water and will walk to other parts of town to buy water or wait until they go home.

If sales decline due to high prices, the State will lose money just like a private enterprise: if the cost of the state's water-selling operation exceeds the income generated by the operation, the State will lose money every day it maintains the operation. The State can subsidize the losses with tax revenues collected from other profitable enterprises (private and government-owned), but this still doesn't make the water-selling operation profitable. It simply means the losses are being subsidized by tax revenues collected from profitable enterprises.

The point here is there are three factors that make work profitable or unprofitable, and thus paid or unpaid:

(1) The scarcity value of the labor (which includes skills, experience, etc.);
(2) The profitability of the employer's enterprise, and
(3) The presence of monopolies that can impose higher prices on the many (i.e. customers) in order to pay higher wages to the few (i.e. owners and employees of the monopoly).

To summarize: enterprises must earn a profit to stay in business—even State-owned enterprises must generate a profit, since every business must retain some profits to invest in replacement machinery and the processes of production. Enterprises can only pay people to perform work that is profitable to the enterprise.

State ownership is no panacea. The State must generate a profit just like private enterprise if the operation is to sustain itself. There are high *opportunity costs* to subsidizing money-losing businesses operated by the State, because there are other things the government could have done with the money other than subsidize a losing operation.

No enterprise, not even one run by the State, can enforce demand on unwilling customers. A monopoly can impose high prices, but only within the limits of customers seeking alternatives or foregoing the product/service.

What makes work profitable or unprofitable?

In general, interchangeable goods and services (i.e. commoditized goods and services) that are produced/marketed by interchangeable workers (i.e. commoditized labor) are low-profit. Both the products and the labor are abundant, so there is no scarcity value.

But scarcity alone is not enough. Scarce skills don't generate profits unless there is demand for those skills.

The only way to make a substantial profit with commoditized goods, services and labor is to maintain a monopoly that enforces an artificial scarcity. But, as we saw earlier, scarcity created by innovation is short-lived, because competitors soon copy the innovations.

The Problem with Monopolies

Relying on profits to generate paid work is problematic for a number of reasons, mainly having to do with monopolies, because, as we've seen above, the only truly reliable way to maintain high profits is to establish a monopoly. But by their very nature, *monopolies benefit the few at the expense of the many*. Monopolies skim income from the many to benefit the elites that control the monopolies.

Monopolies and cartels maintain high prices, which in turn drains income from customers, leaving the customers with less income to pay for other products/services. (High state taxes operate in the same way: high taxes drain income from households, leaving the households with less to spend on private services.)

High prices imposed by a monopoly effectively transfers income from customers to the monopoly, not for better quality goods and services, but simply as a function of artificial scarcity. (This is known as *rentier income*; customers pay higher costs not for more quantity or quality, but because they have no other choice.) Again, households are left with less money to spend on other goods and services.

All monopolies function like the *company store* in *Plantation Economies*, where the plantation workers must buy their goods at the plantation store. Since competition is not allowed, the store can charge high prices, further impoverishing the workers and further enriching the owners of the plantation and its monopolistic store.

As we've also seen, near-zero profit means no one has enough money to hire employees. Even buying automation machinery doesn't generate profits unless the owner of the machinery maintains a monopoly. In wide-open competition, automation tools become commoditized and interchangeable, because anyone else with cash or access to low-cost credit can buy the identical robot and compete with you. The scarcity value of automation tools drops to near-zero, and profits drop accordingly.

Those hoping to "tax the robots" to fund Universal Basic Income (UBI) don't seem to realize that profits plummet with automation—unless a monopoly can be imposed to keep prices high.

The basic problem is that monopoly isn't benign—it comes with high systemic costs. Monopoly means competition is effectively eliminated, or relegated to controlled competition between members of a cartel. This means innovation is suppressed, along with the increased productivity and lower prices resulting from innovation.

The net result of an economic system dominated by monopolies, cartels and guilds is a stagnant *Plantation Economy* in which whatever paid work and profits are generated are hoarded by elites. In such a system, economic stability comes at the cost of innovation, flexible adaptation and widely distributed opportunities for paid work and profitable small enterprises.

Such a system seems theoretically stable, but this is true only if there are no inputs from outside the system—in other words, it is a closed system where no energy is imported, no goods are manufactured elsewhere, no digital labor is performed remotely by people outside the system, no capital leaves the system for higher returns elsewhere, and so on.

But closed systems are difficult to maintain. Few regions have everything they need to maintain a high-cost system of monopolies benefiting the few at the expense of the many. Just as the beachgoers went elsewhere for their water once the State increased prices, people in closed monopoly-dominated systems will find work-arounds to high prices and limited goods and services.

So how can we generate paid work for all in a system that relies on profits to fund paid work? The short answer is we can't.

- In wide-open competition, profits drop to near-zero. Innovation can provide quick, short-lived jolts of high profits, but these are quickly eroded as competitors copy the innovation.
- Monopolies protect profits, but only by sacrificing competition, innovation, increased productivity and widespread opportunities for paid work and profitable enterprises.

Limits on the State Paying for Unprofitable Work

Many observers think the way around this reliance on profits to generate paid work is for the State to hire everyone who cannot find paid work at profitable enterprises. This is a mainstay of conventional Keynesian economic theory, which famously promotes the benefits of the State paying unemployed people to dig holes and then fill them—in other words, meaningless *busy-work* or *make-work*, a category that many now term *BS work* to denote the workers' awareness of the meaningless of their work.

As noted earlier, the State can only collect taxes from enterprises that generate profits substantial enough to pay taxes and employ workers who then also pay taxes. This is why the State prefers monopolies and cartels to wide-open competition: only monopolies and cartels generate reliably substantial profits and employee payrolls which the State needs for its tax revenues.

The State can pay people to do unprofitable work, but as noted previously, the State must subsidize this work by taxing profitable enterprises and their employees. There is an *opportunity cost* to paying people to perform unprofitable work; what else could the state have done with those funds? What more productive uses for the money were passed over to fund the make-work program?

Keynesian strategy calls for the State to borrow as much money as is necessary to pay millions of people to do work that enterprises—private and state-owned—cannot do profitably, on the assumption that any period of mass unemployment will be brief. The theory holds that all those temporarily getting paid by the State to perform make-work will spend their paychecks, kick-starting growth in the private sector that will then re-hire workers to perform profitable work.

But automation and commoditization are transforming the economy by systemically pressuring profits and profitable work. Paying unemployed people to do unprofitable work with money borrowed from future taxpayers is not a solution if profitable work is in structural decline. As I explain in my book *Why Our Status Quo Failed and Is Beyond Reform*, for the state to borrow immense sums every year that accrue interest that must be paid by future generations is not a fiscally sustainable or moral strategy in the long-term.

There is no historical evidence to suggest governments can borrow or print essentially unlimited amounts of currency as a long-term strategy. Ignoring the limits of tax revenues, resources, the debauchery of the currency (also known as inflation or loss of purchasing power) guarantees the eventual collapse of the limitless borrowing-printing scheme.

A New Mode of Production

It's painfully obvious to objective observers that we need a new *Mode of Production*, one that extracts resources more sustainably than the current system, organizes capital, labor and production differently than the current system, distributes income, wealth and capital differently than the current system and presents different incentives to all participants.

The advocates of Universal Basic Income reckon the solution is to distribute profits skimmed from the owners of robots to every adult so they can consume the wealth generated by robots. These assumptions are profoundly false. Stripmining the planet to support even more unsustainable consumption, all in service of a Mode of Production devoted to maximizing profits, is not a solution.

Commoditized robots producing commoditized goods will not be profitable, for all the reasons outlined above. Replacing human labor with robots simply accelerates a destructive Mode of Production, and the initial burst of profits generated by replacing human labor will quickly fade as overcapacity destroys the value of what's produced.

UBI and automation simply accelerate an unsustainable and profoundly perverse Mode of Production.

Those committed to the current Mode of Production naturally claim that it can be reformed into a sustainable, just system by adding Universal Basic Income to the existing system. In other words, they claim that the current system can generate more of everything—more credit, more lending, more consumption, more profit, more tax revenues—and thus there is no need for a new Mode of Production.

But as we've seen, this is wishful thinking. The current Mode of Production will collapse and be replaced with a new system. If we design this new system wisely, it will be far more sustainable, equitable and humane than the failed system it will replace.

Section Two: Money

The Limits of our Social Construct of Money

What Is Money?

What is money? We all assume we know, because money is a commonplace feature of everyday life. Money is what we earn and exchange for goods and services. Everyone thinks the money they're familiar with is the only possible system of money—until they run across an entirely different system of money.

Then they realize money is a *social construct*, a confluence of social consensus and political force—what we agree to use as money, and what our government mandates we use as money under threat of punishment.

We assume that our monetary system is much like a Law of Nature: since it's ubiquitous, it must be the only possible system. But there are no financial Laws of Nature for money. In the past, notched sticks served as money. In other non-Western cultures, giant stone disks (*rai*, a traditional form of money on the island of Yap) and even salt served as money.

In our experience, 1) money is issued by a government or central bank (i.e. a *currency*), and each of these *currencies* is the sole form of legal money (*legal tender*) in the nation-state that issues the currency; 2) each of these currencies is available in physical coins and paper bills and digitally as entries in bank and credit card accounts; 3) our currency is borrowed into existence by the central bank or by *fractional reserve* lending in private banks, and 4) this currency meets all of the utility traditionally required of money:

1. It is divisible into smaller units, i.e. a dollar is divided into quarters, dimes, nickels and pennies, or it is a small unit (for example, the Japanese yen, which is roughly equivalent to a U.S. penny).

2. It is secure, i.e. everyone can't just print or make their own in unlimited quantities.
3. It is fungible, meaning all the units are interchangeable.
4. It is easily transportable.
5. It has a market value that's easily discoverable, so buyers and sellers can confidently exchange it for goods and services.

But history informs us that money doesn't have to be issued by governments, nor does it have to be borrowed into existence by banks, nor does every form of money have to satisfy all five requirement; it's possible to have multiple forms of money which each serve different purposes.

In other words, our system of money is merely one of many possible systems of money. With the advent of digital cryptocurrencies, the range of monetary systems has expanded greatly.

We tend to look at money as value-neutral and apolitical, but as a social construct, it reflects specific social and political values. As I've explained in previous sections, our money is created and distributed at the very top of the wealth-power pyramid. This feature of our money optimizes the accumulation of wealth and power in the top of the pyramid, and thus our social contract of money guarantees the concentration of wealth and thus rising wealth-power inequality.

To understand why, we need to start with money's three basic functions.

The Functions of Money

As a general rule, money is:
1. A store of value (i.e. it serves as a reliable repository of wealth);
2. As means of exchange between buyers and sellers;
3. A tool for recording transactions of credit/debt (i.e. it facilitates recording transactions and keeping track of credits, debts, assets and payments).

Modern-day government-issued currencies perform all three roles. The U.S. dollar, for example, acts as a store of *purchasing power*, a global means of exchange, and as a tool to keep track of transactions, debts and financial assets.

But in other social constructs, different kinds of money perform different functions. The giant stone disks on Yap (*rai*) are a store of value, and a means of exchange for high-value items. But the recording of transactions involving the rai is done in an oral-history ledger: the transfer of ownership of a particular rai is recorded in the community memory, and so the heavy 2-meter-high stone doesn't have to actually move in physical space to transfer ownership. As a result, a stone rai resting at the bottom of the lagoon is a perfectly functional store of value and means of exchange.

The rai are quarried on another island, and not easily counterfeited. They are not necessarily interchangeable; the value of each one is recorded in the oral record. But since a rai isn't divisible, or easily transportable, another form of money is used for day-to-day transactions.

The point here is there is no intrinsic reason why the three primary functions of money have to be satisfied by one single currency.

Nor is there any intrinsic reason why one form of money has to be equally tradable for all goods and services. In some cultures, certain forms of money hold symbolic value and are used solely for transactions of symbolic import, for example, as a wedding dowry.

We assume money has been stripped clean of symbolic or moral value, that it has no connection to anything but its current market value. Yet once again, there is no intrinsic reason why money must be stripped of symbolic or moral value. That our money has no symbolic or moral value is entirely a result of our specific social construct.

In cultures with forms of money that aren't issued by a government, social consensus defines what serves as money and what functions it fulfills.

Our Money System Enforces Inequality

In the modern era, money is issued by governments or their central banks, and this control is imposed by force: if you violate the currency laws, you will be prosecuted and imprisoned.

In other words, our social construct is a *manifestation of power*: the government demands that we use its currency, which it creates and distributes in a process that concentrates income, wealth and power in the hands of the few at the expense of the many. This result not a random side-effect of our monetary system—it is *the core feature of our monetary system*. There is actually no other possible output of the way our system creates and distributes money other than rising wealth and income inequality.

This asymmetry of outcomes (the wealthy and powerful get richer and everyone else competes for the crumbs) explains why the monetary system must be enforced by the State: if the system benefitted all equally, everyone would choose to use it out of self-interest. There would be no need for the State to enforce the system on its citizens.

The saying *good ideas don't require force* expresses this principle: ideas that are self-evidently fair and just will be adopted voluntarily. Only intrinsically unfair and unjust ideas must be enforced, as they reward the few at the top of the wealth-power pyramid at the expense of everyone below.

There's another saying about money: *bad money drives out good money*. This is known as *Gresham's Law*. If there are several forms of currency in circulation, and one loses purchasing power, i.e. its value in the marketplace drops, people will hoard the currency that is holding its value (good money) and quickly spend the depreciating currency (bad money).

Over time, the bad money drives the good money out of circulation as the good money is hoarded.

Gresham's Law poses a problem for States that impose a monetary system on their citizens that fails to provide a reliable store of value and a means of exchange. Even if the State demands the citizens use its money, once that money loses its purchasing power, people hoard other forms of money and get rid of the State's money as quickly as possible: bad money drives out good money.

In theory the State can outlaw all other currencies. But the State is powerless to impose a market value on money it has debased by over-issuance. No seller of goods and services will exchange his valuable goods for currency that buys next to nothing. If the State attempts to force sellers to accept nearly worthless currency for their valuable goods, the sellers will stop growing food, manufacturing goods, etc., for it makes no sense to sell valuable goods for worthless money; anyone who does so will quickly go broke.

If a failed State outlaws other currencies, people become quite ingenious about what can act as money. They start using cigarettes, packages of instant noodles, prepaid mobile phone minutes, etc. as money. In repressive States that enforce the use of rapidly depreciating money, black markets inevitably arise as the only means of enabling mutually beneficial trade between buyers and sellers.

As a result of technological advances—the Internet and cryptocurrencies—there are now forms of money (for example, bitcoin) that can be traded online by buyers and sellers (peer-to-peer networks). The black market for currencies has thus moved online, making it very difficult for States to ban the use of competing currencies.

(Even if a State made a massive and thus prohibitively costly effort to prohibit every cryptocurrency transaction within its borders, there are ways of conducting trades outside its borders, or evading the online surveillance by placing the cryptocurrencies on USB drives that are exchanged in person.)

History informs us that even the most repressive States cannot force citizens to use nearly worthless currency, for the simple reason that producers soon close their doors. Once there are no goods and services being produced, the economy collapses and the State collapses with it.

Author Edward Luttwak drew an important distinction between *force* and *power*. Force is costly and difficult to apply. As Napoleon is purported to have said, "Do you know what amazes me more than anything else? The impotence of force to organize anything."

Imagine coercing 100 reluctant people to use the State's nearly worthless money. The only way to accomplish this would be to monitor each individual, and every location they might visit to exchange money for goods or services, and impose severe penalties on everyone caught violating the statutes by using cigarettes, prepaid phone minutes, bitcoin, etc. for money.

The costs of this surveillance and enforcement are astronomical.

The point is that force is limited by its very nature: the costs of applying force everywhere soon bankrupt the State. Power, on the other hand, works by persuading people to comply of their own choice. Stiff penalties may set examples for others, but ultimately the State's monetary system must serve the needs of the citizenry. If the State's money is not a store of value and fails as a means of exchange, the economy collapses, regardless of how many penalties the State metes out.

How can the State force every farmer to continue to grow food that he can only sell for nearly worthless money? Will the State sell him the seeds and fertilizer he needs in exchange for the nearly worthless currency? If so, what is the State going to use for money to buy the seeds and fertilizer? Certainly not its own currency.

You see the point: no economy can function if goods and services must be traded for currency with near-zero value. The black market that uses other currencies is the only way an economy with a failed currency can function.

The State can only maintain its monopoly on the issuance and distribution of currency by maintaining the utility value of the currency. We obey the State not because it is forcing us, but because obedience is the practical choice.

So while the day-to-day definition of money is "whatever the State issues as money and enforces as the sole legal tender", this State power doesn't extend to the purchasing power of the State currency: the State can mandate a value, but it can't force producers to sell goods and services in exchange for currency with an artificial valuation. This places limits on the power of the State's monopoly.

The Key Characteristics of Our Social Construct of Money

Let's list the key characteristics of our current social construct of money.

1. All money is issued by governments (which include nominally independent central banks).

    This is not a necessary feature of money: money can exist independently of States and central banks. In the modern era, cryptocurrencies such as bitcoin are issued by a decentralized computational mechanism, not by a State, and the bitcoins are valued by supply and demand in the marketplace rather than by a government.

2. Most of our money is digital, i.e. held in financial institutions or online wallets as digital entries. Cash is a modest slice of total money supply—roughly 10% in the U.S., and even less in other nations. Many nations—notably in Scandinavia—are phasing out cash, either to avoid the high transaction costs and risks of robbery cash entails, or to limit black market tax evasion.

3. State-issued money is not backed by anything tangible. In other words, States don't peg the purchasing power of their currencies to gold or some other commodity; each currency is only worth what the global marketplace for currencies dictates via supply and demand.

    We call State currencies "fiat" money because they are created by fiat, i.e. by an act of will, not by buying gold or some tangible asset and then issuing currency in lieu of the asset.

4. Governments can *print* money, either by issuing more paper currency or digital money, but the majority of money in our system is borrowed into existence and is thus debt-based: somebody owes interest on the newly created money.

   When a central bank wants to increase the supply of money, it creates digital currency and uses this new money to buy Treasury bonds and other financial assets such as mortgages. The new money is a debit, while the bonds the central bank now owns are a credit.

5. When the government needs more money to pay expenses above and beyond what it receives in tax revenue, it borrows the money by selling sovereign bonds. This process of borrowing money so the State can spend more than it collects in taxes is called *deficit spending*.

   The State must then pay the buyer of the bond interest for the duration of the bond, and return the principal (the face value of the bond) when the bond matures. So when someone buys a $10,000 10-year Treasury bond, the U.S. government pays the bond holder interest annually, and returns the $10,000 at the end of the 10-year period.

6. Private-sector banks create money in the same fashion: they lend it into existence.

   In the minds of many, banks lend out the money that people deposit as savings. If people deposit $1,000 in savings accounts, the bank can loan out some percentage of that and keep some for reserves—to handle withdrawals and losses incurred should a borrower default on his loan.

   But this is not how it works.

   In reality, the bank actually keeps the $1,000 in cash as its reserve, and originates a mortgage of $20,000 (20 times the reserve) based on the calculated assumption that only a few mortgages will end in default, and that withdrawals by depositors will only drain a small percentage of the bank's total cash reserves.

This system of creating $20 of new money for every $1 in cash reserves is call *fractional reserve banking* because the actual cash reserves are a fraction of the loan.

This system works fine until loan defaults pile up, which causes bank losses to pile up, depleting the reserves, or if there's a *bank run* where a large percentage of depositors demand their money be returned to them in cash.

The money that was created by the new loan goes directly to the borrower. (In the case of a home mortgage, the borrowed money goes to escrow, which distributes the cash to the seller of the home.)

Just as money is created out of thin air, it also disappears into thin air.

When the $20,000 mortgage is paid off, that $20,000 winks out of existence. That's the key attribute of debt-money: it's borrowed/lent into existence, and it ceases to exist once the debt has been paid off.

The interest rate paid to borrow money into existence is the critical feature of debt-money. As we saw in our early example of the beachside water-bottle vendor, his ability to borrow a large sum of money at a low rate of interest enabled him to establish a monopoly on the beach because he was the only vendor who could buy a bottling machine at a low rate of interest. This privilege meant his monthly interest expenses were modest enough that he could lower his costs of production (thus driving his competitors out of business) and still reap substantial profits.

Consider how this dynamic concentrates wealth and thus political power.

A private bank can borrow fresh money from the central bank at very low rates. (Why does the central bank loan money at near-zero rates to private banks? Because the central bank seeks to expand private lending to generate growth in the economy and higher bank profits, which in turn bolsters the banking sector against losses that pile up in recessions and financial crises.)

The private bank borrows money at, say, 1% and then lends it to credit card holders at 16%. This means it earns a whopping 15% on money it doesn't actually hold as cash. It borrows low and lends high. Thus the privilege to borrow low and lend high is literally a license to print profits.

As I noted in the Introduction, if I have the privilege of borrowing $1 billion at 1%, I can then buy a bond yielding 3% and pocket the difference: $20 million a year. That's quite an income for doing no work, making no new products and creating no new services.

In the conventional view of our economy, thrift was required to save money that could then be invested. In this framework, interest-yielding assets such as Treasury bonds were purchased with hard-earned cash that was saved up through years of sacrificing consumption in favor of saving. This savings was not debt-money; the holder of the cash didn't owe interest on this saved wealth.

But our current financial system no longer operates on this traditional framework. The State, banks, global corporations, financiers and super-wealthy individuals can borrow immense sums at rates far below what average wage-earners have to pay. This gives the institutions and wealthy at the apex of the wealth-power pyramid a monumental built-in advantage when it comes to buying income-producing assets such as rental properties, farmland, factories, bonds and financial instruments.

- If the wage earner must pay a 5% mortgage rate to buy a house for rental income, and a financier can borrow 100 times more money at 3% interest, the financier can outbid the wage earner for rental housing.

- If the wage earner outbids the financier for the property, his higher borrowing costs mean his monthly expenses may be so high that he actually loses money on the rental property. A financier makes money on similar properties purchased at the same price due to his lower borrowing costs.

Over time, these seemingly insignificant incremental differences in interest rates can accrue into enormous differences in interest paid and total net income earned on the assets. This is how the wealthy banks, corporations and financiers who have the privilege to borrow vast sums at low rates of interest get to the very top of the wealth-power pyramid —not just the top 1%, but the top 0.1% or even the top .01%.

In a similar fashion, the same incremental advantages characterize our tax system. Earned income—wages, salaries and bonuses—are currently taxed at a maximum of 39.6%, while capital gains from investments are taxed at a much lower maximum rate of around 20%. Over time, that difference yields a substantial advantage to those who collect capital gains—unearned income—from investments rather than from their paid labor.

If we put all this together, we find that our monetary system creates and distributes new money in the very top of the wealth-power pyramid.

You and I can't borrow money from the central bank (the Federal Reserve) at 1%, and this puts us at a systemic disadvantage. We have to borrow money from banks at much higher rates, channeling much of our income to the banking sector. And since we can't borrow at low rates or leverage collateral into nearly limitless lines of credit, we can't buy productive assets as cheaply as those closest to the money spigot.

The result of this system is painfully predictable: the few at the top with access to low-cost credit own the vast majority of the stocks, bonds, business equity, rental real estate and family trust funds.

This enormous income and wealth disparity has a secondary consequence: the wealthy few have tremendous political power, because they are the only ones who can afford to make large campaign contributions and buy all the other tools of political power.

The consequences of the way our credit-money system is structured are stark: by creating and distributing money at the top of the wealth-power pyramid, the system ensures rising wealth to the privileged few, whose purchase of political influence then corrupts democracy.

There is no other possible output of a system that creates and distributes money at the top of the pyramid, and grants the systemic advantages of low interest rates to the wealthy and powerful.

Why Money Loses Purchasing Power, a.k.a. Inflation

Let's return to the basic question: what is money?

Our money doesn't have any intrinsic value like gold coins, and it's not created by decentralized systems like cryptocurrencies. In our system, money is issued by the government and loaned into existence by the central bank and private banks. We've just seen that this system creates and distributes money to the top of the wealth-power pyramid, not to the bottom.

Increasing the supply of money doesn't create more wealth or purchasing power; only the production of more goods and services increases wealth. Creating more money actually reduces the purchasing power of all existing currency, as a larger supply of money chasing the same amount of goods will cause the price of those goods to rise as the result of supply and demand.

If the State suddenly adds a zero to all its currency, increasing the number of monetary units by a factor of ten, it doesn't mean everyone is suddenly ten times richer. It simply means the stock of money has been massively diluted, and therefore the purchasing power of the currency has also been diluted.

The net result of increasing the stock of money ten-fold is that a loaf of bread that used to cost $5 will cost $50.

The State/central bank has the power to devalue its money at will, either by proclamation or by slow erosion from inflation (loss of purchasing power) triggered by increasing the amount of money in circulation at a faster rate than the real-world expansion of goods and services.

Why would a State issue money in such excess that it erodes the purchasing power of all existing currency? The answer is the temptation is simply too strong. The State is besieged by its constituents and favored elites with demands for more spending. Rather than force the sacrifices and trade-offs required to live within the nation's means, the State creates money in excess of what the real economy is producing.

The resulting inflation/loss of purchasing power erodes the value of everyone's income, but note that this erosion is slow enough to be politically useful: it's not enough to trigger any political upheaval, and it eases the State's own debt burdens by enabling the State to pay its interest payments with devalued money.

If this erosion of the currency's value becomes politically destabilizing, the State has several options. It can peg the value of its currency to gold (if it owns enough gold to make this a possibility) or to another more stable currency. Or it can issue a new replacement currency and maintain its value by limiting the issuance of the new currency.

But these actions in defense of the currency's purchasing power come at a steep price: State deficit spending must be severely limited, along with private credit growth. This restriction of deficit spending and credit growth drains the economy's fuel (new credit and State spending), triggering a recession or depression.

The result of State issuance of money and fractional reserve banking is sobering. State-issued currencies tend to lose purchasing power via inflation, as the State succumbs to political pressure to borrow-and-spend and ease restrictions on private credit growth, an action that stimulates speculative borrowing.

All this credit expansion results in increased risk from leveraged loans (loans with insufficient collateral) that inevitably leads to a credit bubble and collapse when the highly leveraged loans default and the lenders do not have enough reserves to cover the massive losses.

In effect, states generate boom and bust cycles of credit/deficit spending expansion that eventually either (a) debauch the currency, or (b) force the State to defend the currency by severely limiting the source of the boom-bust bubbles, i.e. rampant expansion of state borrowing (deficit spending) and private credit expansion.

The inevitable collapse can be pushed forward for a time by ramping up deficit spending and private credit, but this strategy eventually sets up an even larger boom-bust collapse.

Some observers promote the idea that backing a State currency with gold will solve this problem, but this idea overlooks that the key engine of default is credit expansion.

If a private bank can lend out $20 for every $1 of gold it holds, the result is still a boom-bust credit cycle that ends in collapse. The fact that the currency is backed by gold doesn't change the nature of the monetary system at all, as the system is fundamentally a credit-money system of fractional reserve lending.

Others reckon abolishing fractional reserve lending would stabilize the system, but this overlooks the dependence of the entire economy on credit expansion. If lenders can only lend the cash they hold minus substantial reserves against losses, this would cut lending dramatically as net cash savings on deposit is only a fraction of the loans being issued.

What happens to the economy when loans become scarce? One result is households and businesses must start saving more to buy big-ticket items, and the only way to save more is to cut consumption—a move that triggers a recession as spending declines.

In such a scenario, the economy gets hit with a double-whammy: the withdrawal of credit crimps spending on goods and services and credit-fueled speculation in stocks, bonds and real estate. The resulting crash in asset values reduces household and business wealth, which in turn crushes tax revenues and State spending.

The point is there is no simple, easy fix for the instabilities and injustices built into State-issued currency and fractional reserve banking. The only practical solution is an entirely different form of money that isn't State issued or loaned into existence.

Our Reliance on Expanding Debt

Expanding debt is now an essential foundation of our economic system. This begs a question: why?

The answer has several interconnected parts.

The key benefit to debt is that it enables the immediate gratification of desires: rather than have to patiently save up money for months or years, we borrow the money and buy the product today. In economics, this is known as *bringing consumption forward*, as purchases that would have been purchased in the future are bought in the present with credit.

In any consumer-based economy, debt is the essential grease for a significant percentage of consumption. Without debt, consumption would plummet, quickly pushing the economy into recession or depression.

The relationship between debt and energy is a good example of this. As energy analyst Gail Tverberg has explained, energy and debt are deeply intertwined. Now that we've extracted the cheap, easy-to-get oil and natural gas, the costs of extracting, processing and transporting oil and gas are much higher than they were decades ago.

If the price of oil and gas isn't high enough to cover their costs of production and earn a profit, producers lose money. In response, they close costly wells, thereby reducing production. Conversely, if the price of energy is too high, there may be lots of oil and gas produced, but the majority of wage-earners—those whose earnings have stagnated for decades—can't afford to pay the higher prices and still be able to maintain the consumption that the economy needs to keep expanding.

The solution to this conundrum is debt: if consumers and energy producers borrow money, they can maintain their spending/production.

But all this debt creates another problem: as debt throughout the economy rises, debtors must devote an ever-increasing percentage of income to pay the interest due on that existing debt. If the economy isn't generating enough surplus cash to service the debt (i.e. make interest payments), the choice boils down to two unpleasant options: (a) defaulting on existing debt, or (b) borrowing more to maintain the appearance of solvency.

Taking on more debt is the easier choice for most people. Households charge new purchases on credit cards, corporations sell bonds to raise cash, and politicians approve more public borrowing to keep their constituents happy.

The central banks have made this expansion of debt affordable by dropping interest rates to near-zero. (Not everyone gets low rates, of course; many credit cards carry extortionist rates of 15% per annum or more while the banks borrow money at around 1%.)

Still, those relatively low rates throughout the system overall (especially for big-ticket items like mortgages and cars) make it affordable to borrow more every year, and still be able to make the interest payments.

Eventually, though, the cost of servicing this expanding debt becomes burdensome enough that consumption is crimped. Households have no money left after making their debt payments and buying essentials, and government tax revenues are increasingly devoted to interest payments.

The solution that worked in the past—borrow even more so consumption can remain high even as interest payments climb—further crimps future spending, as the cost of servicing expanding debt fuels a feedback loop with no happy ending. When debt expands, it requires even more borrowing to make interest payments and maintain consumption. As this cycle continues, at some point the cost of servicing the debt will exceed the income of households, companies and the government, and the economy dissolves into insolvency as debtors default.

The government can always print money to pay debt, but as noted above, this only devalues the purchasing power of all existing currency. Such devaluation will also eventually bring down the economy as the loss of purchasing power impoverishes everyone.

The reliance on expanding debt is akin to the *Red Queen's race* in Lewis Carroll's story, *Alice in Wonderland*, in which players must run faster just to stay in place: if consumers slow their borrowing, consumption declines. The resulting contraction pushes marginal borrowers into default, and these defaults topple the line of over-indebted dominoes, pushing the system into insolvency.

The Fantasy of a Free Money Machine

The instability inherent in State-issued currencies and fractional reserve banking has led some economists to propose fixes to credit bubbles and busts based on what amounts to a free money machine. Here's how the machine works, according to its proponents:

The federal government (the State) issues $1.25 trillion in new bonds. (This $1.25 trillion is enough to give every household in the U.S. a $10,000 annual Universal Basic Income). The central bank (Federal Reserve) creates $1.25 trillion with just a few keystrokes, and buys the $1.25 trillion in bonds with the newly created money.

The Federal Reserve earns interest on the $1.25 trillion in bonds it now owns, but it returns this income to the Treasury, minus the Federal Reserve's relatively modest expenses of operation. Let's say the bonds carry an interest rate of 2.5%. The State pays the Federal Reserve $31.25 billion in annual interest, and the Federal Reserve returns roughly $26 billion annually, so the net cost to the State of giving every household $10,000 annually is a relatively insignificant $5 billion. (To put this into perspective, recall that the US federal government's 2016 tax revenues were about $3 trillion and its expenditures about $3.5 trillion.)

If this isn't entirely free money, it's extremely close to free money.

Some economists propose a "big bang" one-time payment to every household of $100,000—in other words, a $12.5 trillion issuance of federal bonds that would be purchased by the instant creation of $12.5 trillion in new currency by the Federal Reserve. This $100,000 per household windfall would act as a debt jubilee, in that households with debt would be required to use the one-time gift to pay their debts. Those with no debt would get to keep the entire sum.

In effect, $10 trillion in private debt would be transferred to the central bank. *Presto-magico*, the debt vanishes and everyone lives happily ever after!

But...not quite. As noted earlier, increasing the stock of money while the supply of goods, services and assets remains static *effectively dilutes the purchasing power of the entire stock of money*.

In other words, there is no free lunch. Issuing $1.25 trillion in new money doesn't create $1.25 trillion in new wealth, it simply redistributes the $1.25 trillion *reduction in purchasing power* to every holder of the currency. This free money machine is the equivalent of adding a zero to all currency bills and declaring that everyone is ten times wealthier now. But as we've seen (and history shows), all that happens is a $5 loaf of bread is repriced to $50.

There's another problem with the free money machine. Wealth can only be generated in two ways: (1) by increasing the productivity of machines, factories, computers, software, robots, networks, etc. and the workforce producing goods and services, or (2) by discovering and profitably extracting some new resource—for example, a new oil field that will require a $10 billion investment to extract $100 billion in oil and natural gas; in this example, the $90 billion in net surplus would be new wealth.

Simply adding new money to the system—either with new money issued by central banks or by expanding private-bank issued loans— does not magically translate into higher productivity, i.e. assets and labor that actually generate more goods and services.

Instead the additional money dilutes the existing stock of currency, and new loans that fund speculative purchases of assets such as existing houses don't generate new goods and services. The house still has the same utility value as shelter as it did before its price doubled in a speculative bubble. The increase in its market price did not create any new goods and services or increase productivity; the price rise is simply a speculative bubble that eventually pops when overleveraged loans default and credit issuance collapses.

The point here is that there is no such thing as free money, and productivity doesn't increase simply because the State borrowed and spent money or the central bank created another $1 trillion out of thin air. Rather than generate wealth, these increases in debt destabilize the system by encouraging speculative excesses and credit-asset bubbles which inevitably deflate—with devastating consequences.

The Intrinsic Instability of State and Private-Bank Issued Credit-Money

We've seen that states readily succumb to the temptation to create new money out of thin air to satisfy the infinite demands for more state spending. That this profligate debt-based spending destabilizes the entire system is a long-term risk that politicians and policymakers are happy to take for the short-term rewards of re-election.

State issuance and/or borrowing of new money is not a self-correcting system. Given the low incremental cost of borrowing more money to make interest payments on existing debt, there is no incentive to limit future borrowing: the incentives are all for borrowing whatever sum is necessary to keep politically powerful elites happy.

The only limit on State borrowing is crisis and collapse. In other words, only when the state's ability to borrow collapses will state borrowing cease.

The conventional view is that such a collapse is impossible because "the state can always print more money." But as we've seen, if the output of goods and services doesn't rise in tandem with the expansion of money, the monetary system will collapse as the purchasing power of the currency falls.

Private bank lending is also not a self-correcting system. In theory, as defaults mount, banks pull back from aggressive lending, and the system stabilizes as banks absorb the losses and stop lending to marginally qualified borrowers. But as observers such as former Federal Reserve Chairman Alan Greenspan have noted, in practice, the system actually increases lending even as risks of default mount out of competitive pressure to book as much profit as possible.

This is how the directive to *maximize profits by any means available* creates systemic risk.

Speculation driven by cheap, easy credit also increases systemic risk. As assets rise in price, they appear to provide adequate collateral for more debt. If the market value of a house triples from $100,000 to $300,000, a bank can prudently lend the owner a mortgage far in excess of the previous valuation of $100,000. But when the asset bubble bursts and the home's value drops from $300,000 to $150,000, the bank's collateral vanishes, and its losses explode higher.

The public-relations narrative of the credit-money system is that the ability to lend money into existence gives people the ability to buy tools that increase their productivity. If I have access to credit, the story goes, I can replace my low-productivity handsaw with a high-productivity power saw. The expansion of money is matched by an expansion in my productivity that pushes my income up. This higher income enables me to pay the interest on the new loan and still have surplus income to increase my consumption. In other words, everybody wins thanks to the ability to lend money into existence.

This PR story is certainly compelling, but if we look at what people and businesses are actually buying with borrowed money, we find productivity-enhancing tools are just a thin slice of that. Instead:

- Corporations are borrowing money (by selling bonds) to buy back their own stock shares, not to invest in more research and development but to drive the stock prices higher, a move that enriches the top owners and managers.
- Households are borrowing to buy houses and vehicles that do not increase productivity, and taking on student loans for college educations that fail to yield much actual learning in two-thirds of college students, according to the recent study *Academically Adrift*.

Productivity has actually stagnated in the past decade, along with most households' income.

Rising debt is not sparking giant leaps in productivity or output. Instead, rising debt is now a drag on the entire system, as more and more income must be devoted to servicing all this debt.

Since income is stagnating, the only way to keep paying more interest is to borrow more. But as we've seen, this self-reinforcing feedback of increasing borrowing to pay for the increasing costs of servicing debt has only one end point: a crisis in which households and companies can no longer borrow more to make higher interest payments and maintain consumption.

At that point, the system implodes into default and depression. Attempts to print enough new money to maintain the illusion of solvency only ends up devaluing the currency, impoverishing everyone.

In other words, there is no way out of these traps.

Isn't it obvious that we need a new monetary system?

Section Three: A New Relationship between Work and Money

The purpose of this book was to explore our preconceptions about work and money, and understand the necessity of unchaining money and work from the social constructs of our current system.

If we set aside the current social constructs of money and work, what other system beckons?

Let's start with what we've learned so far.

We found that work is central to human identity and well-being, and to the well-being of our communities and social order. We discovered that the way we create and distribute money at the top of the wealth-power pyramid insures rising wealth inequality via the concentration of capital, income, wealth and power. Our system of borrowing money into existence exacerbates wealth-income inequality by extracting interest from everyone who borrows credit-money.

We discovered that this concentration of wealth at the top corrupts democracy, as wealth buys political power: representational democracy is replaced by an auction of political influence in which *wealth casts the only votes that count*.

We found that Universal Basic Income (UBI), the proposed solution to the replacement of human labor by automation, is not the idyllic panacea presented by its advocates; rather, UBI institutionalizes wealth inequality and impoverishes the many while elites hoard what every human wants and deserves: opportunities for meaningful work, positive social roles and capital accumulation.

We found that humans want work that not only offers a secure income but that also provides a source of purpose, meaning, pride, a positive social role, the opportunity to contribute to something larger than themselves and membership in a community that creates social value. Humans don't want just a serf's subsistence from Universal Basic

Income; they want to play a valued role in their community and accumulate capital in all its forms.

We found that work is not only causally connected to income, capital and wealth, but that *meaningful work and positive social roles are themselves forms of wealth*. In other words, meaningful work doesn't just create wealth, it is itself a form of wealth.

We discovered that not all work can be automated; rather *high-touch work* by its very nature cannot be automated, as human interaction is what creates value. We also found that the demand for high-touch services is essentially insatiable, and that in the current Mode of Production, only the wealthy can afford high-touch services which cannot be automated or commoditized.

We discovered that our Mode of Production—the totality of our financial, economic, social and political systems—is profoundly broken and destructive. We found that the two dominant systems of this Mode of Production, the marketplace and the central state, cannot differentiate between profoundly different things, nor can they recognize or fill unprofitable scarcities.

We found that the marketplace only pays profitable work, and the State pays for work with taxes taken from profits and profitable labor, or with money borrowed from future taxpayers (deficit spending).

We found that the current Mode of Production demands the infinite expansion of consumption on a finite planet and *maximizing profits by any means available*, which incentivizes the exploitation of natural capital and people. We further discovered that consumption is now dependent on ever-expanding debt—debt which accrues interest and thus furthers the concentration of wealth and power.

We discovered that commoditization and over-investment in automation don't increase profits; rather, these global forces destroy profits.

The inescapable conclusion is the current Mode of Production is self-destructive and unsustainable, and the only possible output of this system is stagnation and collapse.

The book's Introduction asked: once we understand work and money in the current system, where does this take us?

We can now sketch out the key characteristics of a new Mode of Production that is fair, just, productive, sustainable and advantageous to all.

Good Ideas Don't Require Force

As noted earlier, good ideas don't require force. I am not suggesting that profit-maximizing markets should be banned, or that state-issued fiat currencies should be eradicated. What I'm suggesting is that *these mechanisms will cease to function as intended*, that is, *capitalism will no longer be attractive to capitalists* and *socialism will no longer be attractive to socialists* as the limitless expansion of credit, production, consumption, profits and tax revenues these systems need to exist will vaporize for all the reasons described above.

What I am suggesting is that a new decentralized Mode of Production with sustainable structures for creating and distributing money and facilitating labor and commerce will be adopted because *these alternative structures function to every participants' benefit* rather than just to the benefit of few at the top of the current wealth-power hierarchy.

The Role of Cryptocurrencies in a New Mode of Production

Cryptocurrency is the first new form of money in 300 years, since the rise of central banking in the 1700s. As I write in late 2017, cryptocurrencies have only been in the public sphere for eight years, and it's impossible to forecast their future role in commerce.

But what we can say definitively is that cryptocurrencies enable new forms of currency that are not issued by central banks and states.

We can note that cryptocurrencies need not conform to the existing social contract of what constitutes money. For example, it's easy to imagine a system in which a variety of cryptocurrencies co-exist, each serving different functions of money and different markets.

We can also imagine different mechanisms for the creation and distribution of cryptocurrencies. In my previous book *A Radically Beneficial World: Automation, technology and Creating Jobs for All*, I proposed a *labor-backed cryptocurrency*, a currency that would be issued to groups and individuals who created new goods and services within their communities to address local scarcities.

In effect, the new currency would be backed by the production of new goods and services that are intrinsically valuable, but not necessarily profitable.

A current example of a cryptocurrency that is created and distributed by a decentralized, opt-in mechanism is Steem, a cryptocurrency that is created and distributed within the SteemIt platform by members who publicly attribute value to content via voting and curation.

A proliferation of cryptocurrencies that can easily be exchanged for a variety of other currencies, each serving different audiences and needs, would facilitate localized community economies that were also part of global commerce networks.

We are still in the early days of cryptocurrency development and innovation, and since good ideas don't require force, those cryptocurrencies which enable decentralized, transparent commerce and the filling of local scarcities that are unprofitable for profit-maximizing corporations will create utility value that will attract users.

It is important to note that a *new Mode of Production requires a new form of money*; the existing form of money (central-bank, fractional-reserve credit-money) cannot possibly support a new decentralized

Mode of Production because it is centralized and hierarchical, i.e. created and distributed at the top of the existing wealth-power hierarchy.

A transparent, decentralized, opt-in (i.e. voluntary) Mode of Production requires a transparent, decentralized, opt-in form of money and a transparent, decentralized, opt-in market for commerce.

In other words, a new alternative Mode of Production requires a new social contract for labor, money, governance, consumption, production and the use and conservation of ecosystems and natural capital.

Enabling Sustainable Commerce that Fills Scarcities That Cannot Be Profitably Filled

Scarcities that can profitably be filled by commoditized production will be filled by the existing Mode of Production, i.e. profit-maximizing global corporations.

An alternative Mode of Production must enable the filling of scarcities that cannot be filled by profit-maximizing companies or the central state; as we've found, these scarcities don't even register in the current Mode of Production: a scarcity of positive social roles, for example, isn't even recognized in the current system as a scarcity or even as a category of scarcity.

Commerce explicitly imagines voluntary trade that is beneficial to both buyer and seller and to the larger community in which the trade occurs.

If people are paid (via a labor-backed cryptocurrency) to fill unprofitable-to-fill scarcities, these workers will have the financial means to buy goods and services to fill their own household scarcities. The lowest-impact production in terms of energy consumption and ecological burden is production that reuses materials that have already been produced that are near the end consumer.

Once profit has been removed as the sole directive in production, then communities can earn money by radically reducing consumption of energy and energy-intensive goods and services.

Once profit has been removed as the sole guide to how capital and labor are invested, people can be paid to do intrinsically unprofitable but highly valuable work such as restoring devastated ecosystems and rebuilding the vitality of soils and waterways. People can also be paid to fill local scarcities of high-touch services that cannot be filled by profit-maximizing companies.

In the new alternative Mode of Production, the sustainability of production and consumption is the prime directive, and the priorities guiding the investment of local labor and capital focus on addressing local scarcities regardless of their profitability. Those scarcities that can be addressed sustainably and profitably will naturally be filled by local or global enterprises. What's different is that scarcities in social cohesion, positive social roles and opportunities to build capital will not only be recognized, they will be filled by the new Mode of Production.

The Outline of a New Mode of Production

We can now sketch out the principles of a new alternative Mode of Production:

- The system must guarantee opportunities for secure, meaningful paid work to all, not a subsistence income (UBI). These opportunities must include access to capital in all its forms and the means to accumulate capital in all its forms.

- All work that fills scarcities in the local community is meaningful and valuable, as whatever is scarce and in demand is valuable.

- While the private-sector marketplace will continue to address whatever scarcities can be profitably filled, the community must have the means to permanently organize and pay for work that addresses local scarcities that are not profitable to fill.

- In other words, the new system must be free of the *tyranny of profit* mandating that only profitable work will be paid and what is not profitable will be left unpaid and undone. The new system must pay people to perform useful, needed work that isn't necessarily profitable in their communities.

- To avoid the domination of the financial elites that control the centralized issuance of credit, this unprofitable but useful work in communities must be paid with *decentralized money* that isn't borrowed into existence, meaning that there is no interest accrued by those who receive this new money.

- This new decentralized money must be distributed to those at the bottom of the wealth-power pyramid who are generating goods and services that fill scarcities and needs in the local community economy, as opposed to the current system that only creates and distributes money in the top of the wealth-power pyramid.

- This new decentralized monetary system only issues new money to pay people at the bottom of the wealth-power pyramid to perform useful but not necessarily profitable work in their communities.

Note that this new decentralized money cannot be issued or controlled by the State, as State-issued money is distributed at the top of the wealth-power pyramid to banks and financial elites.

We've seen that the way our current system issues and distributes money at the top creates an elite-dominated system of governance in which *wealth casts the only votes that count*. Any centralized political-financial system of self-serving elites with the immeasurable advantage of access to low-cost unlimited credit is inherently corrupt.

- For this reason, the power to issue and distribute this new money must be held not by the State or central bank or private-sector banking, as in the current Mode of Production; the power to issue and distribute new currency must be held by the communities themselves.

- The community organization tasked with issuing the currency as wages must be structured so the work that is organized and paid serves the community by creating goods and services that fill local scarcities.

- The process of prioritizing community scarcities must be a participatory democratic process in which members advocate for their choices and ultimately reach a consensus on which projects are the highest priority because they create the most value for the community.

- Since any one social organization might become dominated by a self-serving clique, the new system must allow for the emergence of new competing organizations within every community.

- This new decentralized debt-free currency is a *labor-backed currency*, as it is issued when new goods and services are created by local labor to fill local scarcities. Unlike the current monetary system, which has no limits on the issuance of new credit-currency by central and private banks, the new system's currency is intrinsically limited to the localized production of goods and services that are specifically directed at filling high-priority scarcities in the community.

- Technological advances now enable a *distributed, decentralized cryptocurrency* that is issued at the bottom of the wealth-power pyramid rather than in the very top. This money is not borrowed into existence (credit-money), so it accrues no interest. Since it isn't centralized, rather than concentrate wealth, capital, income and power in the hands of the few at the top, it distributes wealth, capital, income and power to the many at the bottom.

- Rather than increase wealth-power inequality, this new system distributes wealth, capital, income and power to everyone participating in meeting the needs of their community.

I will not go into greater detail about how such a community economy and labor-backed currency might be structured; I have already described this *Community Labor-Integrated Money Economy* (CLIME) in my book *A Radically Beneficial World: Automation, Technology and Creating Jobs for All*. If you are intrigued by the potential for a more productive and sustainable form of money issuance and distribution of paid labor and capital, I invite you to read *A Radically Beneficial World*.

Social constructs are not Laws of Nature; they are the confluence of State power and cultural habits. Both the power of the State and cultural habits are impermanent and subject to change—change we can channel and control should we choose to do so.

Humanity and the planet we inhabit deserve a system of money and paid work that isn't unfair, unjust, predatory, parasitic, exploitive and destructive. Such a system is now within reach.

Charles Hugh Smith

Berkeley, California

Hilo, Hawaii

November 2017

Printed in Poland
by Amazon Fulfillment
Poland Sp. z o.o., Wrocław